*Investing in
Antique Silver Toys
and Miniatures*

.

Investing in Antique Silver Toys and Miniatures

William G. Jackman

AESOP Collectables
Oxford

AESOP Collectables
An imprint of AESOP Publications
Martin Noble Editorial / AESOP
28 Abberbury Road, Oxford OX4 4ES, UK
www.mne-aesop.com

First paperback edition published by AESOP Publications
Copyright (c) 2011 William G. Jackman

A catalogue record of this book is
available from the British Library.

First paperback edition 2011

ISBN: 978-0-9569098-0-0

The author is grateful to all who have kindly made their photographs
available for printing in this book. Wherever possible he has made
known the source of the photographs in the captions

Printed and bound in Great Britain by
Lightning Source UK Ltd,
Chapter House, Pitfield, Kiln Farm,
Milton Keynes MK11 3LW

Contents

Frontispiece: A Victorian kitchen, equipped with silver toys. *Author's Collection.*

*I dedicate this book
to my three granddaughters
Sophie, Chloe and Kate*

Preface

THERE IS money to be made in investing in antique silver toys, and there is no reason at all that, unlike stocks and shares, they should ever drop in value. Furthermore, it is a hobby that very few people are aware exists, and little is known about the makers of the toys. As a result, there is plenty of scope for investigating the history of your hobby, and for still being able to find some choice silver toys dating back from the seventeenth century right up until the present day. The obvious snag is that the further back one goes the more expensive the toys become.

Interest in making tiny copies or miniatures of items in everyday use dates back thousands of years. It is conceivable that cavemen, not having silver at his disposal, whittled a wooden toy dinosaur for his child. Mankind always seems to have had a yearning and admiration for perfectly formed replicas of the larger full-sized original object, whether it be a picture, a piece of porcelain, glass or furniture, or as evidenced by the 'oos' and 'aahs' one gives when seeing a new baby. It is a built in delight we have of the Lilliputian-sized world we are so intrigued by and admire.

The purpose of giving a toy to a child was twofold: it not only amused the child, keeping it quiet and happy; but was also a learning aid – a model for the child to copy, based on its application by the child's parents or the servants.

Nowadays we can add to this a third purpose: as a collectable and an investment

The craftsmen of the day liked to model items which were often made in their respective trades. Glassblowers would make tiny glasses; exact replicas of the originals, cabinetmakers would make tiny doll's-house furniture, of a standard equal to, if not better than, the full-size original. The making of tiny objects was indeed a craft of love. It was, and still is, a fairytale world, as exemplified by, for instance, Swift's *Gulliver's Travels*, in which miniscule objects are a microcosm of the real thing.

It doesn't matter what type of materials were used in the construction of the tiny replicas. European adults, have, since at least the seventeenth century, taken an interest in tiny toy objects they could display in doll's houses or baby houses.

Although originally intended for children to use, these miniature toy replicas fascinated adults even more – so much so that the child was only allowed to see the interior of the doll's house under the parents' supervision, and with strict instructions that they could look but not touch.

It is the finished tiny copy that intrigues adults and makes them express admiration and childish delight when seeing a doll's house fitted out with tiny copies of what they have only known until then as the real item. One can't help admire the craftsmen that have gone to all that trouble to miniaturise a chest of drawers no bigger than a matchbox, or a fireplace with fire irons and fenders, all made of silver. It is not only children who are fascinated by tiny reproductions they can play with.

The parents sought new toys from the silversmiths, getting them to make something unique, especially for their collection. The gold and silversmiths, meanwhile, soon realised that there was a potential market in making tiny toys, especially in silver and gold, and many silversmiths, especially on the continent of Europe, began to specialise in this demanding craft of toymaking.

It was only the English who used the term 'silver toys' to describe our tiny copies of the original-sized objects. They were made originally as playthings. In Germany they are called *silberspielzeuge*; in Holland, the most prolific producer of silver toys, they are referred to as *zilverspieelgoed*.

This obsession with miniaturising everyday items has not diminished over the years, and even today there is a growing and demanding market, seeking even tinier and more accurate doll's-house toys in gold and silver.

A person who might pass by a silver item such as a teapot in an antique shop would stop and admire and become ecstatic over a miniaturised copy of the same item. It is difficult to say exactly why we are so taken by tiny toys; perhaps we marvel at the skill of the craftsman who has had the patience to fashion a miniature; or maybe the human race is simply besotted with tiny things like babies, puppies and kittens – and baby toys have thus been accepted into the same category, just because they're so cute.

From the history of toy miniatures it can be seen that Holland, Great Britain, France, Germany and the United States have shown a definite interest in tiny toys. However, other countries from time to time have produced the small silver toys, in particular China and Russia, but not in any profusion like the Dutch.

As well as using the term silver toys, which were primarily toys that could fit to scale in a doll's house, there was a second size of toy intended for a child to play with. These are referred to miniatures, or, as the Dutch say, *miniaturesterm*. Some of these miniatures are quite tall, reaching up to a third of the size of the original object they were copying.

Another school of thought is that, as well as making silver toys for doll's houses which, as we have seen, seems to be the collecting prerogative of the parents, the silversmiths made toys in silver, scaled to the size of the child's doll, as if the doll itself were using the toys.

There is proof of this fact in the painting, *A Children's Party* by William Hogarth (1773) where children are seen playing with a seated doll, and, sliding off the collapsed table is a silver tea service, which is scaled to the size of the doll.

Figure 1   Painting by William Hogarth, c. 1730: *A Children's Party*, showing a dog upsetting a child's silver tea set (picture from an unknown private collection).

The doll's-house silver and gold toys became more and more a toy or a collector's hobby for the adult. However, as children liked playing with the same type of items their house servants and parents might use, there was also a market for these larger toys. The Dutch are on record as having produced silver toys from as far back as the late seventeenth century.

Silver toys were developed at least a hundred years before the appearance of the first doll's houses. The first toys on record were soldiers and cannons made of gold and silver, created for the young Dauphin in France in the sixteenth century, although this does not necssarily mean that none existed before then; these early toys were replaced over the years with lead soldiers. There are unfortunately, no examples of these early soldiers, though written records of them do still exist in the museums of Paris and Antwerp. The main silver toys were of the type one would expect to find as household utensils and tableware and are still to be found in the doll's houses in the Bethnal Green Museum of Childhood, London. They were generally less than 1.5 inches (4 cm) high.

Thousands of these tiny silver toys were made in Amsterdam in the first half of the eighteenth century, and many of them are in museums around the world, such as the Philadelphia Museum of Fine Arts; the Museum of Fine Arts, Boston, MA; the Art Institute in Chicago; and the Yale University Art Gallery; or they can be found in wealthy people's collections.

The Dutch in the late eighteenth and nineteenth centuries also made little silver displays, or tableaux of people and animals doing everyday things such as hunting, playing, fishing, walking, watching the theatre and the circus. They also made many kinds of wild animals and birds. In fact there was nothing they seemed to have missed as these silversmiths practised their art of producing a new novelty in silver. It is a delight to see how their imagination has expanded into making sets of coach and horses with and without passengers. They made sleighs, pulled by horses and oxen. The sleighs are often filled with tiny models of passengers and driver and, although the figures are no more than half an inch high, they are dressed in fashionable clothes of the period, and are not just seated in their transport, but carry umbrellas, swords and walking sticks. The Dutch made thousands of pieces, and exported many of them to England.

Today, although a profusion of eighteenth-century Dutch toys is still available, there is a scarcity of the toys made by the well-known master silversmiths whose work now demands four figure sums. This is the same for the two highly regarded English silversmiths of the eighteenth century: George Manjoy (whose first work of 1697 is now attributed to him after being erroneously attributed to other silversmiths) and David Clayton, certainly the highest producer of silver toys of the same period.

The third and definitely the most prolific of silver toys is what the Dutch refer to as *e'tage're zilver*. These are little groups of men, women and children, either solo or in groups, going about their everyday life. They usually stand on little platforms and are about an inch high. There were thousands of these produced and many of the originals are still available, although copies are still being produced today in towns like Schoonhoven in Holland, which is known as Holland's silver city, as there are so many shops selling silver and training schools for up-and-coming silversmiths.

The fourth type of toy produced were not toys at all, although they come into the same category and are very appealing to the collector. They are the sort of miniature display pieces which one would like to keep in a showcase. These showcase models are often intended to be operated by hand, but due to their delicate construction these moving parts were never intended as playthings. They were meant to show the owner how the parts were intended to move, and the clever handcrafted engineering involved in achieving it; there weren't many toys that came into this category. Once again it must be pointed out that most of these toys have been copied as far back as the nineteenth century up until the present time, and apart from the makers' marks (which in the case of Holland are difficult to figure out) the majority of pieces all look very much like the originals. The workmanship is still as perfect as when they were first made 200 years ago.

A great deal has been written and researched regarding the larger pieces of silver, but miniatures and toy silver have been sadly neglected. There seems, however, to be resurgence of interest, not so much by English silversmiths as by countries in the Far East who are capitalising on the collectability of miniatures, using in many cases 800-grade silver. Apart from the figure 800 which sometimes appears, there are no other maker's marks. A great number of silver toys and miniatures are also made in the Far East with the 925 silver grades, although in most cases the workmanship is no better than the 800 grade.

The investor today can take heart that plenty of top-quality antique silver toys are still available, and as they become more scarce, prices will continue to rise. There is no need to buy shoddy, poor-quality silver toys, unless of course they take your fancy.

After all, a collector buys what he likes, although an investor may decide to wait until a better piece comes along. The toymakers of the seventeenth to nineteenth centuries deserve our gratitude for all the skill and technology they put into making tiny silver toys. Their skilful work has in the main stood the ravages of time, and far less of their toys and miniatures have finished back in the melting pot as has been the fate of their larger brothers.

Acknowledgments

I would like to say thank you to the following people:

My editor and publisher, Martin Noble

Silver Vaults, London, www.langfords.com

Miranda McLaughlan, at the Victoria & Albert Museum, London

Amy Taylor at the Ashmolean Museum, Oxford

Lily Canvin at the Christies Assay Office

Holland House of Silver Miniatures, www.silver-miniatures.com

Bethnal Green Museum of Childhood, London

Geffrye Museum, London

The following three eBay sellers who let me use their pictures:

Gwenygems for the toast racks

Rebecca Emms and Edward Barnard for the George III teapot

Mattachewey for the elf with barrel

Finally, I would like to thank my wife Jinty for her paience and understanding.

William G. Jackman
Weston-super-Mare, 2011

List of Illustrations

Note

In the following list, due to the fact that hallmarking on the Continent of Europe was very haphazard and inconsistent when these toys were made, I have entered information which I am either certain is correct in some cases or judge to be correct in other cases.

Abbreviations

AC Author's Collection
ac Date of acquisition
D   Depth
Di Diameter
H   Height
L   Length
M   Maker
P   Price paid

1 A Short History of Silver

THE FIRST monarch on record to show an interest in standardising silver was King John (1167–1216). He brought into the country silversmiths from Germany to work with ours so that together they could come to a conclusion as to how pure silver could be best turned into a workable metal, as silver on its own was too soft and needed something mixed with it to give it rigidity and yet retain its malleability.

It was hoped that by combining the skills of two countries' silversmiths the solution could be obtained. It was found, after the silversmiths had carried out their experiments, that copper was the ideal base non-ferrous metal to alloy with pure silver. It was agreed that the ideal mixture should be 925 pure silver to 75 base copper. Apart from a small break in 1697–1720, these figures have remained the same for hundreds of years, and are still the same today.

Nowadays in England, we pride ourselves on our silver being the best in the world and we refer to it as sterling silver. The English called the German silversmiths *Easterlings* because they came from the east of Germany. Gold and silver coins were also known as Easterlings. Over the years the word has been modified to what it is today – *sterling*. The phrase sterling silver is a recognised standard of high-quality silver. Silver is the most workable of fine metal. It can be beaten into sheets and drawn out as wire. It is so ductile that a troy ounce of silver can be drawn out into a wire 40 miles long. It is a wonderful conductor of heat and electricity and as it is self-sterilising, germs cannot survive on its surface; that is why for hundreds of years it has been used for medical and dental equipment

However, having defined exactly what sterling silver would consist of by law, it was difficult to ensure that all silversmiths complied with these standards and that they weren't tempted to add a little extra copper to the mixture or take a little silver out, human nature being what it is. When the wrought plate went to be melted down for coinage, it was discovered to be approximately 20% short of what the Royal Mint expected.

By the late thirteenth century it was found that new problems were being encountered in this country. In 1238, because of the many frauds that were taking place among the goldsmiths of England, Henry III commanded the Mayer and Alderman of London to select six of the most reliable goldsmiths to watch over and supervise the craft of goldsmiths. When Edward I became king we find them being referred to as *gardiens*. It was their task to assay all silver objects before they were passed from the makers and mark them with the leopards head. They would also go from shop to shop and any vessels of gold or silver that were found without the lions head would be confiscated and returned to the King's Treasury.

The reason for this was partly because late thirteenth-century coins, known as 'pollards and crockards', were being imported to purchase English gold and silverwork. The English silver would then be exported to Flanders where the English silver would be exchanged for double the base rate of coins. The foreigners were buying English silver and gold with coinage that was not silver or gold. To curb this malpractice which was affecting the English economy, new and stricter measures were introduced. When Edward I was approached by the Guild of Goldsmiths and asked that something be done to standardise products made of gold and silver in England, he passed a law called *Statutum de Moneta*, forbidding the importing of foreign coins.

The barons and bailiffs of the port of Winchelsea were ordered in 1278 to search everyone passing through that port, with no exceptions including foreigners, to ensure that they were not carrying any silver plate, clipped coins, or any silver, and that any forbidden good should be confiscated until such time as the offender had answered to the King as to why they were carrying them. It was also a command of the King that no person was to leave the country with any part of silver or gold plate without the King's special licence.

There were many examples of persons disregarding these laws, despite warnings and punishments. It became such a problem that the King commanded that these laws about taking all manner of gold and silver plate, clipped money, or scrap silver in and out of the country be read out by the bailiffs every fifteen days at every port in England. Only the King could give permission for a piece of silver to leave this country. Only he could issue a special licence to allow anyone to take a piece of silver. The Constable of Dover Castle was given the responsibility to see that this law was carried out. Failure to comply could result in a person's death and forfeiture of the wrongdoer's wealth and chattels.

This was not the end of the matter because a later order required that all monies brought into the country be tested at the nearest assayer's office for view and proof. Unfortunately this did not stop the trafficking in illegal gold and silver because it was treated as contraband and hidden away from the prying eyes of the bailiffs, though many were caught and executed.

The law forbidding the taking of silver from the country was read out at English ports every two weeks to warn people not to do it. One couldn't travel to another country and take silver coinage with them without written permission, yet the licence to be able to do so was very hard to obtain. In 1306 when the Archbishop of Canterbury wanted to leave England he was not permitted to take any volume of coinage with him.

The King passed a law in 1300 that all pieces of gold and silver would be struck with the leopard's head to show that it had been assayed, and met the standards of the wardens who controlled the quality of gold and silver ingots. This meant that now the goldsmiths of the realm could be watched more closely to ensure they were only using stock which bore the leopard's head. This was the start of what we know today as the hallmark.

2 Hallmarks on Silver Toys

I T WAS NOT until Charles II came to the throne that English coinage ceased being handmade. Until then, all pieces of coinage were stamped with a hammer and clipped to shape with shears. This was most unsatisfactory as there was no regulation size or weight for each coin manufactured and it became an easy way for anyone who felt inclined to make their own money by clipping a bit off each silver coin. When they thought they had sufficient they would then take it along to the silversmith, who would be willing to pay a good sum for the clippings. Alternatively the clippings could be handed over to a forger who would melt them down and, with a forged set of stamps and die, make their own money.

Silver was in very short supply after the English Civil War, the demand for money was so high that it was more profitable to take one's silver clippings along to a silversmith who would be delighted to pay the value of a coin and sometimes even more. The penalty if one was caught was very severe and usually resulted in branding with a hot iron or being hanged on Holborn Hill where many a criminal finished up.

The Tower of London became the Mint

Horse-driven machines were used to produce perfectly round coins of standard thickness. And an inscription marked around the coins circumference of each coin ensured that there was no chance of clipping the coin without damaging it.

It was unfortunate that the old-style clipped coins were in circulation at the same time as the new ones. This also meant that there was nearly twice the coinage on the streets as was wanted by the Mint. The public didn't want to part with their old clipped type coins, and they hid them away and didn't use any of the new coins that came their way.

4 May 1697 was declared the last day for clipped coins to be handed in. The Treasury, which was then in Whitehall, was the collection point, and ten furnaces were set up to melt the out of date coinage. It was melted down into silver ingots. This collecting and melting down lasted several weeks but it was found that the true value of silver received once melted down was far below the expected value because the silver had been mixed with more than the authorised amount of copper for sterling silver.

The public weren't interested in the new coins and continued clipping pieces from the old currency. They hoarded the new coins; it was far more lucrative to pay for goods with the old coins, and save the new ones. As a result, clipping continued for a long time until all the old coins had been gathered in and melted down.

It was recorded that at one stage £52,000 worth of coinage had been collected in, but once it had been melted down it was only worth half of its proper silver value. People hung on to their old coins until the last day of collection and as a consequence large crowds would gather, trying to ensure their coins made the deadline. New problems arose because the issue of new coins was a very slow process and people who had handed in coins had to wait a long time before they received the new ones. This resulted in a shortage of money everywhere which affected everyone regardless of whether they were rich or poor, and the value of silver continued to rise. As they had no money to spend they had to live on credit – if they could get it.

The standard of silverware had existed from AD 1300 to 1696. However after the Civil War an Act of Parliament was passed which raised the grade of silver on 25 March 1697 to a higher level. This new grade was to be used from that date and all pieces of silver plate had to be stamped with the figure of Britannia. Because of a shortage of silver plate after the Civil War, the goldsmiths started using the silver coins of the realm to make vessels of silver, thus depleting the country's coinage. Parliament was petitioned to stop this misuse of silver coins. This act made the standard for items made in silver plate higher than that of the coinage. This increase in purity for Britannia silver was raised from 92.5 to 95.84 and stayed that way until rescinded in 1720.

The stamp of Britannia replaced the lion passant, which until then was the mark of sterling silver. Another mark was used with Britannia, which was the 'lion's head erased' (meaning that the lion's head had been cut off) and which replaced the leopard's head. This meant the goldsmiths had to use the Britannia silver and stop using the old coinage as their source of silver.

There were other changes to the assay marks. One was the introduction of the year letters, a year earlier than normal. (The year mark was another mark added to the assay marks on silver and it showed the year in which the product was made. This was alphabetical, each letter showing a different year, and each year the style of lettering also changed.) The other was the new maker's mark, which had to be the first two letters of their surname, not their initial as it had been up until then.

The hallmarking of early Georgian silver toys bears the marks of the initials of the toymaker. Some examples of those marks are:

- 1665
- FC 1609
- CK with a mitre above 1686
- WP 1689

In the mid eighteenth century the toymakers were producing toys in Britannia silver, which was a higher grade plate. Their names and dates include:

- Joseph Smith, 1707
- Jacob Margas, 1708
- James Godwin, 1710
- James Morson, 1720

There were at least another ten toysmiths who continued making toys.

Mathew Boulton (1728–1809) produced fine-quality toys from his workshop in Soho Birmingham, and anyone who is fortunate enough to find or own one is indeed a lucky person.

Mathew was in partnership with another very skilled toymaker named John Fothergill. The toys were stamped MB IF in two separate shields whilst both were active. When the partnership broke up in 1782 only the initial MB was used.

According to Birmingham Assay Office there are no registered toymakers in Birmingham today. They did, however, become established in Birmingham between the years 1770–1780. By now many machines had taken over a lot of the hard work in silversmithing of toys. The toymen could now buy and assemble press-shaped units, which they combined together with handmade parts.

Sterling silver came back into circulation in 1720 and Britannia silver continued along with it for ten years. It was then phased out until it was revived for a short while in late Victorian times. The leopard's head replaced the lion's head erased in 1975.

Outside London, the provinces were given the right to have an assay office and stamp their own silver, providing they were producing coins of the realm. Before 1697 many centres used marks. The maker's mark became very prominent, sometimes being stamped on a piece more than once. Date letters were also found stamped by some cities including York.

The Britannia standard of silver was introduced in 1697, although it is unfortunate that no provision was made for its use in the provinces; technically it was illegal for the provinces to mark silver. However they did, and in doing so added greater confusion because they altered the shape and design of the characters they were then using, making them very awkward to recognise even today.

A new Act was passed by Parliament which allowed any city which had a mint to assay stamp their own silver. The Act, dated 1701, allowed Chester, Bristol, Exeter, Norwich and York to stamp silver.

The Act was a very bad mistake because it not only included Bristol and Norwich, which did not have a mint, but excluded from the list Newcastle which was one of the most important cities and one which had its own mint.

Because of these mistakes, particularly in the omission of Newcastle, a new Act was passed in 1702. From that period onwards all towns and cities that required items of silver marked had to send them to their nearest assay office. By 1883 all the provincial towns had stopped using the leopard's head. Only London continued to use it to show that was where an item had originated. It was, and is today, the lion passant which is the recognised sign of sterling silver.

It is interesting to note that the leopard's head was stamped on bars of gold as well as silver and was not confined to London but was used throughout the country. Despite the laws regarding the leopard's head, unscrupulous goldsmiths continued to try and cheat the system by stamping their own leopard's head marks on substandard pieces of silver.

The origin of hallmarks

A law was passed in 1363 that every master goldsmith had to have his own mark which he would leave on any piece he had made so that, in the event of dispute, the man responsible could be traced. The marks were registered and were usually small symbols which were personal to that particular goldsmith. It wasn't until the late fifteenth century that the goldsmith's personal initials were used instead of a symbol. This made his work much easier to recognise.

In 1478 another letter was added which was known as the date stamp, although it was never originally intended to be such, but a means of tracing the assay master should a piece be found to be substandard. As the assay master was changed each May, a new letter was allocated to each one in succession. It is therefore easy to see how the particular letter could be found and matched to a corresponding year. That is how today we are able to trace the year the item was made (unless the hallmark on the silver was a forgery).

3 Dutch Dating Codes for Silver Items, 1815–1960

BEFORE THIS practical system of date-stamping silver was introduced, most towns and cities making toys, such as Amsterdam and The Hague, used their own system of date-stamping their or otherwise marking their work. Date marking with a letter started as early as 1503. For a number of centuries there was no national standardised system, each town guild had its own mark and dating system. The present system was put into place in 1815 and has remained largely unchanged until today (see Figure 2).

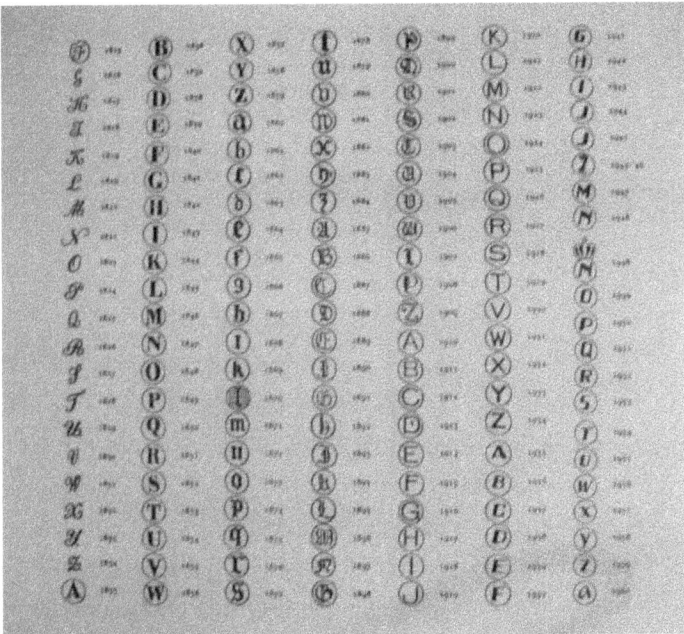

Figure 2   Dutch date stamping system, 1815–1960.

However, a problem arises when toys are found which, though date-stamped, do not register on this chart: because alphabetical codes were used in the eighteenth century there is no record to establish the exact year in which a particular toy was made.

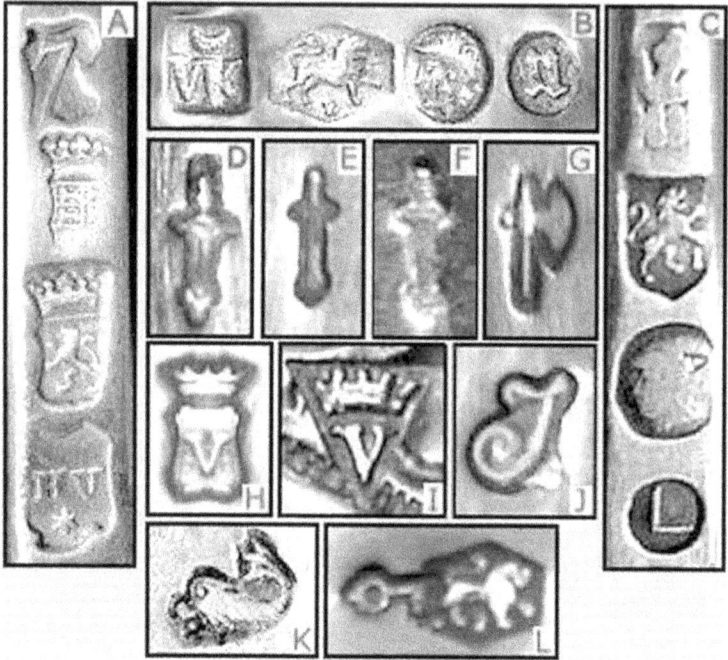

Figure 3   Alphabetical hallmarks.

The hallmarks in Figure 3 are ordered alphabetically. The section marked **A** (left-hand column) shows the silver guild marks used in some 35 of the larger towns in the Netherlands in the seventeenth and eighteenth centuries. They show what one would rarely find in reality, namely all four of the marks, supposed to be on a piece of silver during the period prior to the dismantling of the guilds in 1810. Top to bottom they show:

- Z for date letter mark for 1782
- the Rotterdam silver mark
- Next the lion rampant silver guarantee mark (875)[1] the maker's mark of Vendrik Vrijman.

The **B** marks, across the top of Figure 3, have been used from 1814 to the present day. From the left they show:

- the maker's mark
- lion passant mark
- the Minerva head or duty mark
- the date stamp mark.

The **C** (right-hand column) marks are basically the same as B, except that the maker's mark is unknown. The lion rampant is silver purity .934. The letter L in a circle is the year date for 1921.

D and **E**:   These sword marks were in use 1814–1905 on toys that were too small to take a full hallmarking. They were also used to mark the excess pieces on fully hallmarked objects which comprised of multiple parts.

F This sword mark was in use 1906–1953, in the same circumstances as D and E. From 1953 a similar sword was used, but with the standard silver numerals on the blade of 835[2] and 935.

G is the axe mark, and was in use 1853–1927 as a tax mark for old silver items bearing old silver marks that had come back into circulation.

---

[1] This figure depends on the percentage of pure silver to copper. As the copper content increases so the figure decreases. Regulations in the UK now acknowledge a silver grade as low as 800 parts to 1000. The silversmith stamps the object with the grade of silver it was made of, as long as it is within acceptable limits.

[2] The present standard sword mark on silver shows the figures 835, which is the silver grade used.

H and **I** are tax marks applied to larger articles of foreign silver.

J: The script letter I is also a tax mark for old Dutch made silver. It can be the only letter found on a piece of silver, but does not guarantee anything in particular apart from that of a tax mark.

K: The dolphin mark was in use 1859–1893, for Dutch made articles of silver that were below the 833 purity standard. It was also used in 1893–1905 in a triangular shaped cartouche.

L: The key mark was in use in 1853–1953; it is stamped abutting or intruding on the lion or the sword standard mark to indicate that the object was made for export.

4   The Duty Mark

S ILVER HAS for many years been used to collect tax and help governments swell their coffers. This was the case in 1784 when a new tax was imposed on silver and introduced a new mark on silver which was the King's head, shown in profile. The first king was George III. His head is shown facing to the left, but from 1786 onwards the monarch's head has always pointed to the right. In 1841 when Queen Victoria came to the throne the sovereign's profile once more reverted to facing to the left. It stayed this way until 1890 when the stamping of the monarch's head showing that tax had been paid was discontinued.

The only provincial cities that are assaying outside of London today are Birmingham and Sheffield and they were both established in 1773. Birmingham still uses the anchor as its assay mark and Sheffield the crown. It is said that the two directors of the cities involved were using the Crown and Anchor pub in London as their base whilst waiting for their petition to be heard in Parliament, and, on the spin of a coin, decided between the two of them who would have the anchor and who would have the crown.

The Hallmarking Act   (www.theassayoffice.co.uk)

According to the UK Hallmarking Act of 1973 (amended 1998) it is illegal to offer items for sale described as gold, silver or platinum unless they have been tested and hallmarked by a UK Assay Office. An item may be exempt if it weighs less than 1.00 gm in gold or 7.78 gms in silver. It is also exempt if it weighs less than 0.50 gm in platinum.

Note: There is no weight exemption in the Republic of Ireland, and all items destined for sale there must be hallmarked.

The following information has been offered by Thomas's UK, 36 Sheep Street, Skipton, UK, Diamonds, Fine Jewellers.

The UK Common Control mark for sterling silver is 925 finesse. Silver has a new commercial standard 800; this means that much jewellery and silverware which has previously been condemned as substandard is now acceptable, although it is not of sterling silver standard. This will bring into recognition European silver in the 800/835 grouping which will be hallmarked 800. It is important to watch out in the use of permitted symbols today. The lion passant (rampant in Scotland) is the mark associated with sterling silver, while 958 Britannia silver had a distinctly different mark. It is in the interest of the collector to be on his guard. On silver after 1999 one must look at the purity as a numeral, because the symbols may be confusing.

5 Silversmiths and Their Marks

THE WORKMANSHIP of silversmiths of the past, and in particular their work on toys and miniatures, although very difficult to find today, can still be seen and admired in many famous museums around the world, particularly in Amsterdam, London, and the United States. There are many other museums which have small displays of their workmanship.

There is no mistaking the high quality of the workmanship of these early silversmiths, but without their individual marks one cannot be one hundred per cent certain they were made by a certain individual, particularly as so many toys were copied. Because the toys of the seventeenth and eighteenth centuries were individually handmade it is natural to suppose that each of them was a one-off, that having spent hours perfecting a particular toy or miniature, the craftsman was in no hurry to make another exactly the same and would instead be turning his thoughts, perhaps, to the next project he had in mind. This is especially relevant to the work of master silversmiths like George Manjoy and David Clayton, whose quality of work is excellent.

Even today it is nearly impossible to find information about the famous English silversmiths of the eighteenth and nineteenth centuries. Very few books have been written on the subject, and it is thirty years since Victor Houart wrote his magnificent book, *Miniature Silver Toys*.[3] He states himself that a great deal of research is still needed on the silversmiths of those days and the making of silver toys in England; a subject about which little is known.

---

[3] Victor Houart (1984) *Miniature Silver Toys* (translated by David Smith). London: Random House Value Pub (original French edition, *L'Argenterie miniature*, published 1981).

Despite that fact, collecting tiny silver toys and miniatures is a fascinating hobby. It is apparent from eBay, where many such items sell for hundreds of pounds, that there is a high demand for them. No sooner do good-quality Dutch toys appear than the bidding starts and prices rise. Early English toys of the eighteenth century are so expensive that they tend to stick for weeks without selling. It is possible to buy dozens of eighteenth- and nineteenth-century Dutch silver toys for the price of a toy silver Georgian teapot.

Many of the silver toys are blackened with age and are very difficult to clean, as they are very delicate and if heat is applied (even hot water) it can melt the delicate silver joints of the toy. Most silver toys will never need cleaning if kept in display cabinets and only handled by people wearing gloves. It is the acid from the sweat in the hands which can cause tarnishing. If one has a piece of silver which is particularly dirty the best remedy is to use Goddards Long-Term Silver Pad Foaming Silver Polish. One or two applications of this should shift the most stubborn of stains.

There have been toys for tourists since at least the mid nineteenth century. They were often bought as little silver mementoes. Those pieces made of pure silver weren't cheap even then – and much less so today – but if someone wanted a little keepsake, such as a silver miniature of St Paul's Cathedral or the Eiffel Tower; then these items could be purchased. Today, there is plenty of silver to be found and numerous gift shops and good-quality jewellers sell silver toys.

Many of the countries visited today for the warmth of their sun, for instance in the Mediterranean, now sell silver toys to tourists. Turkey and Greece are forerunners in this profitable business. They are copying little models of Greek antiques, like small pots and vases. Large quantities of these unmarked silver toys can be found on the many islands of Greece. Despite the fact that many countries in the world sell silver toys for tourists, they are of little interest to the true collector of antique toys. They don't have their wares hallmarked or indicate the country of manufacture and investigating the marks found on Dutch and English toys is half the fun of collecting.

The history of silver toys teaches us that the first known toys were made for the children of royalty and it took many years before they were made in great profusion for children in families who could afford them.

6   A History of Silver Toys

THE FIRST REAL record of silver toys being made and given to children was in 1404, when Charles VII of France was given a silver rattle and a silver plate when he was one year old. A generous benefactor in 1571 was Claude of France, the daughter of Henry II and Duchess of Lorraine. She ordered a Paris goldsmith named Pierre Hottman to make her a doll's house with every conceivable household utensil including a set of silver household pots, bowls, plates, 'such as are made in Paris'.

It was her intention to present this as a gift to a child of the Duchess of Bavaria. This proves beyond question that the manufacture of silver toys in Paris at the end of the sixteenth century was very commonplace – certainly for royalty and the wealthy.

There is still in existence a very detailed journal which was the property of Jean Heroard, the physician in charge of the infant Dauphin of France who was later to become Louis XIII. The journal dates from 1601 and covers events in the young prince's life until the death of Jean Heroard in 1628. The journal tells us that the young Dauphin took delight in martialling his servants in the palace around in military fashion. His love of toy war was encouraged to teach him the rudiments of military discipline and warfare.

In his journal Heroard quoted the young Dauphin as saying, when he was only five years old, in a letter written either by him or dictated by him to the King, who was then engaged in a battle with Duc de Bouillon at Sedan in Northern France:

I have been to the Arsenal, Papa. M. de Rosney (Maximilien
de Bethune, Duc de Sully) showed it me full of beautiful arms ...
and he gave me some sweetmeats and a little silver cannon.

The little future king was so besotted with his cannon that he
tied it with a garter to his pinafore so that he wouldn't lose it.
However, it was his grandmother, Jeanne d'Albret, Queen of
Navarre and mother of Henry IV of France, who started the
collection of silver toys in the Bourbon family. It was passed to the
young Dauphine's father, Henry of Navarre (Henry IV) She also
acquired a 'dolls set of silver table plenishments set with diamonds'
This set, along with all the toys of her collection have vanished,
and it is only from her inventory that we know they ever existed.

Silver toys in the sixteenth and early seventeenth century were
made predominantly for the children of kings and princes. Louis
XIII (1601–1643) was fortunate to receive many toys made of
silver. He was given a miniature watch as a present by his mother
Marie de Medici, and in the same year his mother had arranged for
the young prince to have 300 silver soldiers made for him by
Nicholas Rogier, who was gold- and silversmith to the Dauphin.
Some of these toy soldiers were inherited by his son, Louis XIV
(1638–1715).

These were further augmented with more soldiers and
cannons, all of which were intended to teach the young princes
how to practise military manoeuvres. Indeed, the liking for military
artefacts by the young Dauphins continued through several
generations. No cost, it seems, was spared and ten million francs
were spent on a huge collection of silver soldiers and militia.
However, Louis XIV decided to melt most of them down to help
pay for his wars. The sad part was they only raised three million
francs. What a pity there are no toys left from these early royal
collections: all have vanished without trace and only written
evidence is available to show that they ever actually existed.

The manufacture and collection of silver toys has never received high praise or acknowledgement; very few museums have collections, and very little is written about them or displayed in magazines or periodicals. Even books on silver, not specialising on the subject of silver toys, devote only a few pages to the subject. Times are changing though, and today one can see the works of these wonderful craftsmen from years ago.

The Victoria & Albert Museum, London, has acquired a handsome collection of miniatures and doll's houses, but unfortunately they have moved most of these over to the Museum of Childhood at Bethnal Green, London. There is still a small silver toy display, but not as good as it used to be.

The Ashmolean Museum, Oxford, UK, still have a very good selection of silver toys, but because the museums have bought so many collections as they became available, this has resulted in a shortage, so prices are rising for those few early pieces at a ridiculous rate. The majority of collectors today would agree, when asked to pay £2000–3000 plus commission and VAT for one tiny coffee pot, that the prices are far beyond the pocket of the majority of collectors.

The Dutch were surging ahead in the manufacture of silver toys, the most productive period being 1725–50. England was still suffering under Puritanism, a product of Oliver Cromwell's regime, discouraging all fun and games and frivolity. Unlike Holland, we had forgotten how to enjoy ourselves. Any effort made by the English to make toys like the Dutch only resulted in boring tea sets and mundane household furniture, although we were well aware of the toys Holland was making, because they soon started exporting them to Britain. Proof of this can be seen on the import marks stamped on their exports.

According to Charles Oman, Head of Metalwork at the Victoria & Albert Museum, London, and an expert on silverware, 'It is strange how we never even copied them, because the copying of toys made by different silversmiths seems to have always been in vogue' (Houart, 1984, p. 179). As to whether we were skilled enough is beyond question. We just never did copy their work, although English silver toys were equal in quality to those of the Dutch, if not better in many cases, especially the work of George Manjoy. For instance, we go into raptures over the outstanding one-offs made by our top silversmiths; most of which are now in the Victoria & Albert Museum.

When the Netherlands were producing silver toys it appears that their customers were not the men and women of that era, but wealthy royalty, landowners and businessmen, who bought the toys for their own pleasure as well as that of their children's. It was the adults who built up vast collections of silver toys. It is folly to think that every child had a toy box filled with these wonderful fruits of a true craftsman's labours. They were still very expensive, and each one took a long time to make. The conditions the silversmiths worked in, with poor lighting, dusty workplaces and very limited tools, are all the more reason why each toy should be regarded as a work of art and explains why they were – and still are – so expensive.

Today, a tiny George I silver toy teapot one inch high is far more expensive than a full-size, four-piece Georgian tea service. However, the Netherlands did produce thousands of tiny silver toys, and really let their imagination run amok in the ideas they came up with in what to make next.

As there were so many toys being produced in Holland from 1725 to 1750 that they not only satisfied their own market requirements but had to be exported, this makes nonsense of the supposition that these toys were either the work of apprentices or were samples that a salesman would present to a prospective customer who was looking for a frying pan made of iron. Besides, even if this was the case they wouldn't require thousands of them.

Occasionally, Christie's of London do hold an auction of someone's collection, but they are rare. The last one was held on 16 November 2010 and there was little available to the collector under £1000. One item of great interest sold at this auction was a Dutch toy cruet set. It showed the maker's mark of William van Strant, Amsterdam, 1735, who was a highly respected master silversmith. The cruet set was only 7 cm high and the price paid for the cruet was £6000.

Victor Houart, in his book *Miniature Silver Toys*, advises collectors to concentrate on eighteenth-century toys. That was thirty years ago. Times have changed and the market most available to the collector today is that of nineteenth- to twenty-first-century toys, of which there are still plenty available, especially as the museums have not yet decided to buy them. The better nineteenth-century toys are fetching the higher figures and even at today's prices they are still a good investment.

*

The quality and quantity of silver for doll's houses and miniatures declined after 1750, which was the most prolific period of production. Interest wained in the doll's house from an adult collector's point of view, and it became more a plaything of the child. The splendid expensive fittings were mainly being replaced with more mundane practical toys made of German pewter, brass and china. Proof of this can be seen in the Bethnal Green Museum of Childhood, London, where there are lots of nineteenth-century doll's houses.

Although the furnishings of doll's houses were mainly the prerogative of the adult, the original intention was for children to play with them, and many did, though for the majority of children the furnishings were not silver, but copper and pewter.

The doll's houses were made for little girls to play and act the part their mother or maid would play in their own homes. They could be as large as a third of the size of the original item they were representing. These larger toys were also made of silver, though unfortunately very few examples of them exist today. These larger toys were known as the *poppengoeden*.

The Dutch are renowned for their skill in producing large quantities of tiny silver and gold toys of an exceptional high standard. They made every conceivable toy including horses and carriages, dogs and cats. They made frying pans with toy fish in the pan, and grills with meat on, tea services, doll's prams and furniture. Candlesticks were another item high on the list of popular toys. The English silversmiths only produced kitchenware and tableware; and the occasional piece of furniture.

The daughter of Henry II of France in 1556 in a moment of generosity ordered that a selection of silver toys which should include bowls, plates, buffet pots and a large assortment of other items, be given as a gift to the children of the Duchess of Bavaria. It has been discovered that in the plate inventory of the mother of Henry IV of France (1553–1610) she possessed a set of miniature silver dolls toys set with diamonds.

The wealthy children of the United Kingdom were not as fortunate as their Dutch counterparts. They were not privileged to enjoy the pleasure of silver toys to furnish their doll's houses until after the restoration of Charles II in 1660. The earliest hallmarks prove that it wasn't until 1665 that they started to be manufactured in London and it was uncommon for hallmarks of toys made in the provinces to be found.

It was fashionable for the children of wealthy Stuart families to furnish their doll's houses with every conceivable manner of household objects, all made out of silver. These included fire grates, bedsteads, sideboards, commodes, tables, chairs and tea-making equipment and almost everything one would associate with a home in those days. As collections were handed on from one generation to another, and then added to, one could see how a collection would grow and an extensive range could be amassed over the years.

One interesting fact is the close likeness of the toys to the actual items they were copying. This was despite the fact that the silversmiths had to meet budgets and that not everyone could afford the best; the workmanship therefore left something to be desired and the finer details were often omitted to reduce costs.

However there was always a good silversmith somewhere who would not sacrifice skilled workmanship and it was this craftsman that took the range of the toys even further. Miniature figures of men, women, children and babies were put on the market. There were cooks, butlers, and household servants, horses and carriages, household pets like parrots and their cages, cats, dogs, beggars and soldiers. The list was endless. There was nothing that could not be copied in silver to make a toy house as complete as possible.

7   How Silver Toys Were Made

THE SILVERSMITHS in those far off days were not blessed with the tools and facilities they enjoy today. There was no electric light; all they had was candle power and later oil lamps. The buildings didn't have large windows where they worked, and many of the silversmiths had poor eyesight. Yet they managed to produce a complete range of duplicated miniatures. It is difficult to imagine how it was possible for them to hold them as some of the components were so minute. The majority of toys they made were manufactured from thin sheets of silver; small intricate and ornamental pieces were cast and then soldered on.

The final shaping of the tiny components was finished by hand. The toy was only completed when the craftsman had checked it carefully for faults, and polished it to perfection and to his complete satisfaction. Foot-operated lathe turning was available during the seventeenth to eighteenth centuries, so it is reasonable to assume that hollow, round tubular shapes such as candlesticks would be turned in the lathe, cut to length, and other fittings soldered on. Legs of tables could be turned or cast, then finished by hand.

Hand raising was a skill used by the silversmiths. This was a process done with the help of the lathe. The flat plate metal was spun on the lathe and pressure applied to form the flat plate into a bowl shape. It would then be hand-worked from there. George Middleton (1660–1745) was an outstanding English silversmith in his day. He made beds and chairs in the style of those of the Charles II period. Isaac Malyn was skilled at making toy gate leg tables. The tiny gate legs were cast and hand-finished before fitting. Many of the silversmiths specialised in a particular toy or parts of them.

In the Westbrook baby house, in the Victoria & Albert Museum, London, can be found today many examples of toys made by famous silversmiths of the day. The marks on them attribute them to the individual craftsmen who made them. Tiny fireplace sets by George Middleton complete with tongs, firedogs and fender, shovel and poker. Not all the silver toys in the Westbrook baby house are made by the same person. John Deards of Fleet Street (early 18th c–1731) contributed several examples of his work. There is a grate complete with fireback on which the maker's mark can be seen. These initials can also be found on six plates and a mug attributed to him.

Also in the Westbrook house can be seen the work of John Clifton, another artistic silversmith in his day. Again, there is a complete hearth and grate, including all the accessories for keeping a fire going. There are two chairs on which can be found the marks of Mathew Maddon who lived in Lombard Street, London. He registered his work in the Assay Office in 1696.

Thomas Evesdon, another great toymaker of his time, contributed a three-legged silver pot, which was made in 1713. The maker's mark, as it became known, was another addition to the hallmarks required by law to help prevent fraud. In many cases only the maker's mark is visible. This does not always mean that the piece was made by him, but that it is attributed to his workshop. Some toys were so tiny that they might only have the maker's mark on them, and some were excused having any hallmarks because they were so minute, and the impress marks could damage a delicate piece of silver.

Another fine distinguished silversmith was Augustus Courtauld. He registered his mark in 1708 at the London Assay Office, and opened his workshop in Church Street, St Martin's Lane. He was another very fine maker of toys, and produced them in an enormous quantity, considering the limitations imposed by working conditions on silversmiths in those days.

He specialised in the production of toys though his high output meant he had to take on another full-time assistant whose work was of an equally high standard. After 1740 he no longer fully hallmarked his work, but resorted to using only his initials AC, which was his registered silvermark. These can be found stamped two or three times on pieces of his work.

The production of silver toys peaked in the eighteenth century. David Clayton, who only made silver toys, specialised in this field. His work was of such high standard that it was always in great demand and the quality of his work was unsurpassed, except for the work of George Manjoy, a silversmith who was a lot older than Clayton. There is no doubt that David Clayton was the most outstanding toy manufacturer in his day.

The demand for miniature toys made of silver was such that many silversmiths made the manufacture of them an important part of their trade. David Clayton made nothing else. Another silversmith was John Sotro, a craftsman whose work was in great demand in the years 1720 to approximately 1750. He advertised on his business card the fact that toymaking was a large part of his trade. The card read:

Goldsmith and Toyman making all sorts of toys at reasonable rates

In Bath, Cheltenham and several other spas where wealthy people came to take the water, there were retailers of silver toys. One such retailer was Deards, though it is probable that the goods were manufactured in London by the same company who were silversmiths.

The Deards were a popular family of silversmiths in London. A large part of their trade was the manufacture of good quality toys. A succession of family members were engaged in the manufacture of miniature silver toys. John Deards, the man who started the business, died in 1731 and worked in Fleet Street.

Another toymaker whose work was respected was Paul Daniel Chevinex (he registered his mark with the Society of Goldsmiths in 1730). He not only made toys out of silver, but would completely furnish a customer's doll's house in silver toys the way they wanted it.

Entered in Sir Ambrose Heal's *London Goldsmiths*[4] are listed the goldsmiths of London and there are about 7000 names, However, there are only 30 described as 'toymen'. This is despite the fact that toys were very sought after. The skill in making them was limited to the specialists. Any toys one might find with hallmarks of George II – or even better George I – should be treasured as they are rare and very valuable.

---

[4] Sir Ambrose Heal (1972) *The London Goldsmiths, 1200–1800; The London Goldsmiths, 1200-1800; a Record of the Names and Addresses of the Craftsmen, Their Shop Signs and Trade-Cards. Published Under the Patronage of the Worshipful Company of Goldsmiths of London.*
Newton Abbot: David & Charles.

8 Dutch Silver Toys

THE HISTORY of the Dutch hallmark is much more complex than the English hallmark system, in that they never adhered to the rules regarding what should be marked on their finished pieces of silver. It appears that silversmithing was crafted in Holland about the mid seventeenth century. There is no denying that the first early toys on record were made in France and Germany, but their silversmiths did not continue to do so; in fact, many of them came to Amsterdam to continue making toys. The doll's house also became popular in Holland in the latter half of the eighteenth century and there is no doubt that it was this that caused the adult population to collect silver toys to decorate their doll's houses, which became their pride and joy.

It wasn't until the late fifteenth, early sixteenth century that legislation was issued by, first of all, Archduke Maximilien, and later in 1503 by Phillip IV (Philip the Fair) that silver and gold products should become hallmarked. This was obligatory and all were expected to comply by marking their work with their own individual mark. The easiest one to recognise today is the Amsterdam mark which consisted of three small 'x's with a crown on top, inside a rectangular escutcheon. This mark is very common and was used by many smiths to denote their toys to show they had been made in Amsterdam, when in fact they hadn't been, so one needs further evidence before being sure that what they have is a treasure toy by a distinguished maker.

It is possible to overlook a silver miniature made by a famous silversmith of the day because he had not stamped it with his mark, or because he didn't comply with the changes of legislation on silver marking, and continued mixing the old mark of a personal symbol, like a rabbit, a deer or a tree, with his initials. As a result, many eighteenth-century pieces are unmarked but are recognised as being antique. It is worth looking out for the date code letters, usually boldly stamped on the toys. They are generally in alphabetical order and changed each year. This was used to show the year of manufacture.

This practice has been in use since 1528. The Dutch lion rampant was another mark which had to be added as from 1663. This brought the total to four statutory marks that had to be made on pieces of gold or silver. A collector would be fortunate to find a toy with all four marks. Many silvermakers only left the town mark, and there were those that left nothing. Considering there were so many silversmiths operating in Holland only a few are known with a reputation for greatness, though most of the others, many of whom are unknown, were skilled craftsmen.

One of the early silversmiths whose mark is worth noting is Pieter ter Haer. His mark was a sand glass in an upright oval. A very concise display of Dutch hallmarks and the name of the silversmiths to whom they belonged, can be found in Victor Houart's book *Miniature Silver Toys*.

Dutch hallmarks

One will find when inspecting pieces of Dutch silver – apart from vague makers' marks and year dates which are impossible to trace – tiny individual sword marks. There are basically three of them. The smallest shows the piece was made between 1814 and 1905; the larger one shows it was made between 1906 and 1953; the third and largest sword has a number (usually 835) showing the silver grade dates from 1953 and this is still in use today. It is important to know these as it will save hours of exasperation trying to find if a toy is by a well-known maker and worth a four-figure sum. The other mark which tells you straight away if the toy is scarce is the dolphin stamped on it. This mark was used on gold and silver from 1859 to 1893.

The making of silver toys was not limited to Amsterdam. In fact the outlying towns, or Frisian towns of the Low country of Holland, were producing silver toys well before Amsterdam, but because of lack of knowledge collectors and connoisseurs have not rated these towns and their silver work with any degree of importance.

There is a school of thought that Leeuwarden (the capital of these Frisian towns) was actually producing silver toys in the sixteenth century. This, according to Victor Houart, is not true. Yet it is surprising that these little villages in a rich agricultural area, of no great importance to tourists, did manage to manufacture miniatures, in silver, of the tools and implements they used in everyday life. There must have been a local demand for these miniatures from local people who could afford to buy them.

In the Ashmolean Museum, Oxford, there is an excellent example of Dutch doll's house silver, especially in the Lady Henriques collection (see below, Figures 107 and 108, p. 106). This is in contrast to the Victoria & Albert Museum, London, which has very few tea drinking toys, and whose silver toys tend to be larger. These were undoubtedly meant as playthings for children, or glass cabinet display toys, which were not to be played with.

9 Doll's Houses

T HERE IS NO record as to who built the earliest doll's house, but there is an inventory of one that was made in Nuremberg for Albrecht V of Bavaria in 1558. It was originally intended for his daughter but when it arrived he decided that it was far too nice a toy for her and put the house in his own art collection. The doll's house would almost certainly have contained toys made of silver.

It was roughly 50 years later that doll's houses of German design started taking shape. Christopher Weigel is known to have written in 1698.

> *The materials of which these dolls and playthings are made are in part silver and are fashioned by gold and silversmiths. [...] Indeed, there is scarce a trade in which that which usually is made big may not often be seen copied on a small scale as a toy for playing with.* (Poliakoff, 1980, p. 7)

The desire of adults to buy doll's houses started in Germany, spread to Holland and fifty years later became established as an English hobby, primarily for adults, or so it is assumed.

In England, during the eighteenth century, the doll was already established as a child's baby, so that when doll's houses appeared in England they were called baby houses. There are many superb examples of doll, or baby, houses in the museums of the United Kingdom. There is a fine collection of baby houses or doll's houses at Bethnal Green Museum of Childhood, London. In fact the Westbrook baby house which was once in the Victoria & Albert Museum has now been moved to the Bethnal Green Museum.

The wealthy Englishmen returning home from the continent brought with them the Dutch ideas of having portioned cabinets standing on legs, out of range of sticky-fingered children, where the adults could view and keep their treasured possessions. These cabinets were similar to the Dutch doll's house, except their doll's houses had two doors on them that when shut made them appear to be ordinary wooden cabinets. When the doors were opened all was revealed, a dazzling display of decorated and furnished rooms in the Dutch style. Those owned by the wealthy folk were furnished with gold and silver household fittings, while the lesser well off had to be content with brass and pewter.

In England, the tall secure cupboard for hiding adults' treasures eventually had to give way to 'squatters', as children's tiny dolls moved in. It was only a matter of time before the English doll's house as we now know it came into being with its elaborate front of house decoration and opening out to display equally tastefully decorated interiors. These early doll's house were usually locked, as many contained expensive silver furniture fittings, kitchen implements and utensils. Around 1700 the English decided it would be nice to have their baby houses with a full frontal view like an ordinary house with doors and windows, and so the modification began to what we recognise today as a doll's house.

In the Geffrye Museum in London, there is a surviving doll's house of the early proto type Dutch design, owned once by John Evelyn (see below, Figure 5, p. 62). These houses were exact replicas of actual houses of that period.

There was no limit to the extremes the owners would go to make their particular doll's house as authentic as possible. The doll's house of Petronella Oortman, built c. 1690 and now housed in the Rijksmuseum, even has silver displayed in her doll's house cupboards, exactly as a bride would have her dowry. The money spent on furnishing these houses more than suggests that these doll's houses were used extensively for amusement by adults.

Figure 4   An early Dutch doll's house, c. 1800. *Courtesy of Bethnal Green Museum.*

Figure 5   John Evelyn's doll's house in Geffrye Museum, London.

The purpose of the original doll's houses was educational, particularly in the kitchen. In 1631, Anne Koferlin not only had a doll's house built but fitted it out as a training module. She published an explanatory leaflet teaching the future housewives the value of the kitchen components and how they were to be used.

It seems the attraction began to build from what was intended as a training aid, into an adult collectable hobby. Many women took pride in their baby houses and took them into marriage as their personal treasure. Once again England followed Holland which had their doll's houses about fifty years before England did.

The arrival on the scene of doll's houses in Holland and England justified the excitement of collecting silver toys. It was somewhere to put them, and it gave a purpose and justified the expense. With thousands of toys being produced in Holland, far more than they required for their own need, they exported toys to England. Germany, France, Holland and England were on good trading terms at that time, although in England we were making some toys our selves.

In the early eighteenth century the Duchess of Schwarzenburg created a baby house she called 'Mon Plaisir'. It consisted of a hundred rooms and was supposed to represent daily life at court. Some ladies were so obsessed with their doll's houses that they spent more money than they could afford on them. The ladies took their doll's houses with them when they married, and continued building their collections. Frau Negges in Augsburg spent so much on her doll's house that she financially damaged her estate. Arnoldus van Greffen and Frederick van Strant were the most prolific of the silver toymakers in Amsterdam at this time of the surplus. There is no doubt about it that as described on trade cards of that period, silver toys were being exported to London and Paris.

The English baby houses were a little later in becoming established in comparison to the Dutch, and they were smaller than the Dutch doll's house. Despite the size of the houses, there were plenty of silver toys in England. The question is: what happened to them? Where did they go? There must have been at one time hundreds, if not thousands, of silver toys, including those we made ourselves and those which were imported from Holland,

We have in England our own baby houses, one of the most famous being the Westbrook house or Killer house, so named because it was donated by Mr Killer to the V&A Museum (see below, Figure 6, p. 64). It was built by tradesmen on the Isle of Dogs, London, and given to a small girl, Elizabeth Westbrook, as a present in 1705. A large handsome oak cabinet standing on its own six legs, it is decorated in the fashion of an eighteenth-century wealthy man's house, and is fashioned in that style. There are many

pieces of silver toys in it, including beds, fireplaces, pots, pans and
kettles.

Figure 6   Westbrook doll's house, showing the kitchen with silver miniature
pots hanging on the wall. *Courtesy of Victoria & Albert Museum.*

Figure 7   The Victorian lounge in my doll's house, using 25 pieces of silver
from my own collection which are a mixture of English and Dutch
pieces. Total value today: £900.

Jonathan Swift, the author of *Gulliver Travels*, confirms in his story in 1726 how the Queen of Brobdingnag ordered for Gulliver furniture for his convenience in his room. Gulliver goes on to relate:

> *I had an entire set of silver dishes and plates, and other necessaries which in proportion to those of the queen, were not much bigger than those I have seen in a London toyshop for the furniture of a baby house.*

This interest in doll's houses was helped along by the collection of Queen Mary who presented her own doll's house to the Museum of London. Queen Mary was also fortunate to be given two other doll's houses, one being Titania's Palace. This was given to her in 1922. This doll's house was until recently on loan to Wookey Hole Caves in Somerset where the public was able to see it. The other was a doll's house given to her by the nation in 1924 and designed by Edwin Lutyens (1869–1944). An eminent twentieth-century architect, he was commissioned by Princess Marie Louise, a granddaughter of Queen Victoria, to build a doll's house for Queen Mary who was a very keen collector of the 'tiny craft'. He gathered together the finest painters, silversmiths and skilled craftsmen to create what was known, when presented to Her Majesty, as 'Queen Mary's Doll's House' and which is still on display to the public at Windsor Castle. This house is the better of the two and contains a very impressive collection of very fine authentic Georgian silver toys from that period.

The doll's houses themselves made excellent display cabinets. Apart from Holland and England, very little miniature silver was produced in the eighteenth century. America produced some silver toys. There is an eighteenth-century doll's house in which there is a covered dish made by Peter Biermann in 1709. The doll's house is in the Historisches Museum, Basle.

When equipping a doll's house with furniture and tableware, even when keeping the objects to scale, the tableware was very tiny, yet items of furniture were made of silver and were naturally much larger, but still intended for the doll's house. This is seen in the Westbrook doll's house which is equipped with silver beds, fires complete with irons and tongs etc., wardrobes, tables, chairs and every item of kitchenware imaginable that was in use in the seventeenth to eighteenth centuries.

In other countries that made doll's houses they didn't have a problem, as they didn't fit their doll's houses out with silver furniture. The German doll's houses, which were filled with pewter and copper utensils, were used as training aids, to teach girls how a house should be laid out and the utensils that were required to furnish it. The fittings in the doll's house depended on the wealth of the owner as to whether it was brass and pewter or silver. The wealthy Hapsburg family had gold utensils in their doll's house.

If proof were needed that the doll's house was first and foremost a training aid then witness the following letter written in 1765 by a Mr Paul von Stetten:

Concerning the training of maidens, I must make reference to the playthings many of them played with until they were brides, namely the so called Baby Houses.

It was quite normal for many of the young brides to take their doll's house into their marriage, and continue to collect silver toys. Unfortunately, few pieces of German silver remain that are not already part of a museum doll's house. This makes it appear that they were solely intended for this purpose.

There is even an example of a doll's house made in the same style as the Dutch ones. It was a present from Queen Anne to her goddaughter Ann Sharp.

10   English Silver Toys

THERE IS little evidence of the making of silver toys in England before the Reformation. King Charles II lifted the gloom that seemed to cover the land under Cromwell's control. People felt enlightened, and more inclined to spend money on such silly things as silver toys.

The English system of marking silver had gone through many changes, but with the introduction of silver toys and miniatures even more confusing regulations were added. It must have been bewildering with so many toys being imported, some marked, and others marked with a variety of silver marks, none of which made much sense. Added to this we had the mix up caused by our silversmiths changing their own marks and not registering them. Furthermore, one of our silversmiths decided to use the same initials as another. Next the maker's surname had to be shown and from around 1720 legislation demanded that in addition the initial of his Christian name also had to be displayed.

It proved a grave mistake when in 1739 a decision was made to stop stamping miniature silverware. Some silversmiths continued to mark their wares with their initials. It is unusual to find English silver toys dating from the nineteenth century hallmarked, but as we didn't make many of our own during this period, it is of no great consequence.

We know that there were toymakers in England in the seventeenth and eighteenth century. There were also silversmiths. What we don't know is which silversmiths were toymakers. It is also very perplexing as to what English girls and women did with all the silver toys accumulated in this country, not only those pieces we imported but also those we made. Very few of them are to be found today from that period.

So many pieces of silver toys were produced and so few now remain that one wonders what happened to them. English doll's houses were much smaller than their Dutch counterparts and much less luxuriously furnished, and the English doll's house was used more by children than the Dutch ones, but there is no doubt that we did make silver toys and import many others. Evidence of this can be seen by the import marks on Dutch toys for sale over here.

Because of the hallmarking changes of 1697 and post 1720, several great names have found to be incorrectly attributed to one man who actually never made a single toy. That man was George Middleton (1660–1745).

There is some confusion regarding the marks of George Manjoy and George Middleton. According to the latest research, work stamped MA should be attributed to George Manjoy, as should work marked GM. He marked his work (of which there was a great amount, all of the highest standard) GM. On top and below of this were embossed a number of crescents. This is the written view of Victor Houart but it conflicts with the view of several earlier authors on this subject who rank George Middleton as the finest English toymaker.

It is left to the collector to research further the whys and wherefores of this argument. So many silver miniatures and silver toys were attributed to this man Manjoy. This point is made because many collectors will want to include at least one piece of his work in their collection. His work was only superseded by that of David Clayton, who was years younger than he was, and is another indispensable name to have in one's collection of silver toys.

Clayton too is involved in a mix-up over initials used in his maker's mark. But David Clayton did register his own initials, and stamp hundreds of pieces of his own work, and some he imported from Holland. There was another silversmith with the name of

Clayton who may have been the son of David. This man was John Clayton. It is fair to warn the collector that these early silver toymakers did nothing to make the recognition of their name stamp on silver very easy. There is a great deal of contradiction regarding to whom the initials really belong – but this is all part of the fun of collecting. There are many books available with makers' marks of this period.

This has shortened the list of those who actually were tiny toymakers. Further to that fact, it was discovered that the numerous toy porringers that were about were not actually porringers at all; they were too large for doll's house and were in fact *dram cups* – little silver cups with two handles to be used by adults for taking a dram from. They were not toys but we can't be certain of their exact use. There have been many suggestions – for instance, they may have been cups from which to eat porridge or from which to drink (adults only) or may even have been designed as bowls to hold sweet smelling herbs to counteract against the evil smells of the day. Whatever they were, they weren't toys, and plenty of them were made.

It is also worth looking out for small mustard spoons. There were hundreds made over the years but some of them would fit the category of silver toys, or miniatures because of their size. There are three well-known silversmiths of the eighteenth century who made spoons: James Tookey, John Robinson and John Holland. It is quite possible to find copies of these today because there are so many mustard spoons. The lengths to watch out for are 73 mm and 82 mm. They should be marked with at least the maker's initials.

There is little evidence that silver toys were actually sold direct to the public; instead they were retailed in shops. During the late eighteenth century there were large imports of mass-produced iron toys from Germany. The question of what use the British made of their toys still remains unresolved. As time went by the demand for tiny silver toys diminished. The doll's houses in England were beginning to fill with German pewter imports and English ceramics seem to take the place of once popular silver items such as tea services and flower vases. As the market peaked in its general retail trade so interest in silver toys waned. The wealthy population needed better items on which to spend their wealth. A collection of silver toys in a doll's house was no longer of interest. The shops were becoming full of full of lavish, tempting goods for the consumer. Lady Mary Wortley Montagu referred to a shop in Bath in a poem she wrote in 1736:

> *Farewell to Deards and all the toys,*
> *Which glitter in her shop,*
> *Deluding traps to girls and boys,*
> *The warehouse of the fop.*[5]

This is a comment by a consumer referring to the changing fashions in the market, in particular the collection of silver toys for children which were passing out of fashion. Not that there is any record that Deards in Bath actually sold silver toys as we know them, but the *silver toys* in the sixteenth and seventeenth century did not necessarily mean 'toys' in the true sense of the word, but silver buckles, vinaigrettes, buttons, snuffboxes, patchboxes and an assortments of other silver oddments. By the mid eighteenth century London had seen the best of the silver miniature and toys.

The Dutch continued to make toys, and England produced very little in the nineteenth century, although during the mid to latter period the manufacture of toys did recover a little. This recovery continued and the twentieth century saw better toys than before coming on the market. A good example is the unmarked *linen press* which is a copy of one by Daniel van Strant of

---

[5] Lady Mary Wortley Montagu (1736) *Farewell to Bath*, ll. 13–16.

Amsterdam, 1754, which sold at auction at Christie's on 16 November 2010 for £1200.

It was also becoming recognisable that children were themselves becoming the new up-and-coming market, and consumers in their own right. In 1740 John Newbury published books especially for children. This was followed twenty years later by the dissected puzzle for children, which was a forerunner of the jigsaw puzzle.

Silver miniatures were still produced in both Holland and England during the nineteenth century, although most of them were copies of earlier times. A little town named Schoonhoven started a revival of the silver toy trade. The town not only started producing toys in great profusion but began training schools for up-and-coming silversmiths as they still do today. Eventually the adults tired of doll's houses, cheaper replacements for silver toys took their place and the interest died – until now, when silver toys are once more in vogue and a good investment.

It wasn't until the Victorian era that a desire for silver toys was resurrected. Even then they were much bigger than the earlier Georgian toys. An exhibition of Queen Mary's treasures, held in the Victoria & Albert Museum in 1954, showed a silver toy tea set from this period.

The Victorian silversmiths were renowned for embellishing early antique silver pieces, large and small, with their own style of decoration. It seemed they just couldn't bear to look at an authentic Georgian piece of silver which had not been decorated without embossing it with some designs or pictures which they thought increased its beauty when in actual fact it decreased the value of the item, often by at least half.

This is very evident when one looks at early English silver toys and miniatures. There is no evidence that Dutch miniatures made in the eighteenth century had ever been embossed with cherubs or crawling babies, but there is plenty of evidence that

English silversmiths seemed to delight in importing selected pieces and embossing them with playful mischievous naked babies and cherubs.

It wasn't until the Edwardian period that the desire for making and collecting toy silver pieces really caught on once again.

There was a revival of Queen Anne and early Georgian period due to the revival for silver toys shown by Queen Alexandra. Such was the demand for early reproductions during this time that the prices of these toys rose at a tremendous rate, as they are still doing today. According to Houart (1984) early collectors of eighteenth-century toys together with museums and other private collectors around the world have caused this continual increase in demand and increase in price. Houart advised people to collect pieces from the nineteenth century because of the ever-increasing prices of eighteenth-century pieces. There is one well-known Birmingham firm named John Rose Ltd who were very much involved in the production of toys and the same dies are still in use today. The interest in tiny silver toys and miniatures was such that Birmingham silversmiths were exporting toys back into Holland and other European countries.

Victorian silver toys and miniatures are still available today on the Internet, but the demand for them is rising daily, as are the prices. One or two nice pieces are for sale but the collector must be prepared to pay three figures for them. As so many dealers are now trading online, the chance of finding these toys in flea markets are getting less. The antique fairs of Great Britain do seem to hold a good selection of toys and miniatures, but you need to look hard in their glass display cabinets to spot them.

The collecting of silver toys is a comparable unknown hobby but there are some real bargains to be found if the collector is aware of what he or she should be looking for. One of the big advantages of collecting silver toys and miniatures is the fact that you are unlikely to find that they are damaged, or have been repaired or have been faked to make them look like what they are not. Generally speaking, silver toys remain in very good condition, even though they were made over 300 years ago, because they were mostly locked away in doll's houses and only attended to by responsible adults. They were made by skilled craftsmen who took pride in their work and produced toys of quality which were meant to last.

Moreover, if a part has come adrift and has had to be repaired it is very difficult to hide the fact that soldering work has been carried out as it always leaves a dark stain. There were so many toys in circulation that there was no need to counterfeit them. However, toys were copied, and still are today. The copies are very good and of such high standard that the perpetrators could just have easily made their own. Unfortunately, the silversmiths responsible also punched false hallmarks on the pieces. This has caused additional confusion in trying to ascertain who actually made what. The hallmarks on silver toys, in particular the Dutch ones, are so small that even with a magnifier it is very difficult to be certain who made most of them. It was as if the maker were coy about marking pieces clearly and didn't want to advertise the fact that they had made it, even though it was a requirement by law.

Scarcity of silver during the Napoleonic period, together with the fact that many toy silversmiths had been recruited to fight in the wars caused a shortage of skilled craftsmen. The result was that during this period there were fewer silver toys in comparison to those made in the Georgian reign, and there were not so many of them. Some silver toys were produced in the provinces, but they were of little importance. Most of the English silver toys and miniature pieces were made in London.

The revival of silver toys was very slow in the early nineteenth century. Very few pieces of miniature silver are to be found in this period and any that were made have disappeared into private collections.

Miniature silver toys can also be found in the Ashmolean Museum, Oxford. There is on display a collection of silver toys that is part of the Lady Henriques Collection. One can see a three pronged fork and knife. This has the Sheffield hallmark 1832 though at an average of four and half inches long they were not suitable for a doll's house.

There were many lady silversmiths during this period, some of them made silver toys. One such lady was Sarah Bowman, of Queen Street, Sheffield, who is attributed with the making of toy teapots and mugs.

11   The Present and Future of Silver Toys

DESPITE THE FACT that gold and silver prices are rising daily, the amount of silver toys being produced today is far more than it was a few years back. The majority of modern toys are foreign imports from many different countries, and although in days gone by the collector wouldn't have given a piece of silver not made of 925 purity a second glance, times have changed. The Assay Office has decided to recognise this standard of silver so there are more toys becoming available of that standard.

These toys are bright, they lack the patina of older silver toys, but they are well made, and the maker doesn't seem to skimp on silver. They will be the antiques of tomorrow. The fact that some countries make their toys in lesser grades of silver than ours is of no great consequence because countries like Germany have been doing it for years and have produced some fine toys, though not a lot. The crossbow shown in Figure 80 is marked 800 silver, which I am sure any collector would agree is a fine prize to have in one's collection.

There are some good quality toys coming from Italy, Malta and Greece. Most are marked with the silver grade, if nothing else.

Miniatures encompass many different silver items, including the larger ones used for children to hold and play with as they did hundreds of years ago. There are now available very smart coloured enamelled pill boxes in 925 grade silver. These boxes are well made and very attractive and have been seen for sale in street markets at prices ranging from £12 to £45.00. Where they were made is a mystery as they have no assay markings on them apart from the silver grade. Still, they are attractive and will in due course become a collectable and an investment.

The modern interest in collecting silver miniature toys has produced many attractive copies of Georgian originals, and some toys that are very modern and have never been made before, such as motor cars, tractors, aeroplanes and bicycles, just to mention a few. It means that even now one can start a collection at today's prices, which are very reasonable. There is also a very large range of silver pendant charms coming on the market in every conceivable design. These were never intended to be classed as toys, but apart from the ring attached to them, that's what they look like and now would be a very good time to start collecting them.

It appears that one can expect many kinds of silver grading now that the British have relaxed their standards from sterling silver. There are many different grades, ranging from 800 to 950 silver, some of which were, up until recently, not classed as acceptable standards.

It is good to see that the production of silver toys has not lapsed. The demand is getting greater every year and silver prices are rising so that it makes sense to invest in these charming collectables. There is no evidence that we in England are today making them in any great quantity, but Canada has a Little Dollhouse Company with a very active toymaker and silversmith who is producing first-class doll's house silver toys at very reasonable prices.

Their shop and factory, at 612 Mount Pleasant Rd, Toronto, Canada, is open every day of the week and accessible online at http://www.thelittledollhousecompany.com. They have been trading for 35 years and have established very high standards both in making and selling doll's houses and all that goes in them Not only does their silversmith Don Henry manufacture toys in silver he also makes them in gold.

12   Buying Silver Toys as an Investment

C HILDREN'S TOYS of silver and gold were not the privilege of wealthy English children until after Charles II came to the throne in 1660.

Today these toys are still available but compared with twentieth-century copies they are very expensive. The asking price on eBay for a George III miniature silver teapot today is £2300.

Like all goods that are desirable, as the shortage of them becomes more acute, so the price rises. Items of silver are still being manufactured today, and the standard is very high. Now is the time to start collecting. There is little known about Dutch and English silver toys. They are easy to recognise as being antique. They are too small and delicate to falsify makers' marks, yet thousands of them were made and the dealers are becoming aware of what is desirable and scarce. As the eighteenth-century toys and miniatures become more and more scarce and expensive so the collectors will turn their attention to the nineteenth- to twenty-first-century toys.

For the collector there is another advantage: the toys are small, take up very little space and don't require any cleaning. They haven't been tampered with (not yet).

Today one is able to buy a larger range of miniature silver items including motor cars, ships, aeroplanes, houses, bicycles and a huge assortment of animals, birds and fishes. There is a great demand for cats and dogs, and also owls are very popular.

Top dealers are always being asked what the next collectable will be. Why shouldn't it be silver toys and miniatures? Perhaps everyone is waiting for someone to bring a boxfull along to BBC1's *Antiques Road Show*. Many pieces have hallmarks on and many more don't. The scarcity of the toy does affect its value, but the fact that the Victoria & Albert Museum has one just like it will no doubt increase its value. Copies of Dutch toys are starting to come on the market but they look so clumsy and amateurish that only a fool would not recognise them for what they are.

Although it is highly desirable to own a silver toy on which the collector can recognise the maker and when it was made, this should not be a barrier to owning it until something better comes along.

A collector is very unlikely to come across a toy from Holland made of any metal apart from silver, even though the toy may be as black as jet due to the dirt, and soot it has been exposed to without ever being cleaned.

A serious collector can find out the going rate for many toys if they concentrate on the sales at the major auction houses. Christie's in London will oblige and help a collector. They may advise you where there is an auction with silver toys coming up for sale. The Victoria & Albert Museum even has its own book, detailing the story of Dutch and English toys.[6]

It would be a good idea to visit the London Silver Vaults[7] in Chancery Lane to see fine examples of silver toys that are very beautiful and not very expensive. The Silver Vaults is a row of underground shops which sell nothing but silver. It is most impressive and the silver dealers are very helpful.

---

[6] Miranda Poliakoff (1980) *Silver Toys and Miniatures*. London: Victoria & Albert Museum.
[7] London Silver Vaults, 53–64 Chancery Lane (corner of Southampton Buildings), London WC2A 1QS (tel: +44(0) 20 7242 3844).

13 Where to Find Silver Toys

SILVER TOYS and miniatures are not hard to find. And just like hundreds of years ago, a collector can if they so desire buy a doll's house and try and equip it with as many silver toys as they can find. Go to county antique fairs and flea markets. Look in the tabletop glass display cabinets, hidden away in a corner of small antique shop; it is quite likely that you will find a piece you are looking for – and they are certain to be under lock and key.

There are to the best of my knowledge no books available today (that are not out of print) covering the subject of silver toys and miniatures. Two well-known books which are very good and still available on the secondhand market and on eBay are:

- *Miniature Silver Toys* by Victor Houart (prices vary from £25 to £175, depending on condition) – the information is excellent but it was published in 1981 in the United States and details are sketchy after the early twentieth century; also prices are not in euros.
- *Silver Toys and Miniatures* by Miranda Poliakoff – again out of date, but it describes beautifully Dutch silver and doll's houses that used to be on show at the V&A

As a result of a visit to the Silver Vaults another book of great interest to the collector of silver toys has been brought to my attention. Unfortunately it is written in Dutch, but there are many pictures in it of silver toys and makers' marks. It is called *Klien Zilver, 1650–1880*.[8]

It is certainly worth travelling to the main English museums which display silver toys. This will help familiarise the collector of

---

[8] B.W.G. Wttewaall (1987) *Klien Zilver 1650–1880*, Amsterdam: A. de Lange.

what to look out for, and the names and makers' marks of great silversmiths of England and Holland. The reading will further enlighten the collector of museums of interest and places to visit in Holland which is only an airbus ride away.

Try eBay on the web (www.ebay.com) and search for **Solid silver miniatures.** Be patient. It may be a few days before something tasty comes on view but the excitement of winning a bid is like a tonic to the collector.

Go to the Victoria & Albert Museum in London and the Ashmolean Museum in Oxford; look at the tiny silver toys, and get to recognise them. Search out the doll's houses at these museums and others mentioned in this book (see also Appendix I: Museums to visit (UK)). Remember, hundreds of silver toys and miniatures had no silver at all yet are perfectly authentic. Get to know the hallmarks of the top half a dozen Dutch silver makers. Their work demands four figures. Get to recognise the same of the early English silversmiths; their work too demands four figures. Read, learn and study the toy market. It's fun and rewarding.

It is also interesting for children; they can associate with them and even at a young age take an interest in toys that were produced hundreds of years ago. It is quite reasonable to imagine that one needs a lot of money to build up a silver collection, yet this is not necessarily the case. However, there are so many pitfalls that an unsuspecting collector can fall into when buying items of silver that for the majority of everyday collectors for whom this book has been written they will be well advised to:

1. buy from a reliable dealer;
2. purchase small interesting pieces they can afford;
3. get a signed receipt;
4. search the Internet.

Today there are nowhere near the variety of pieces that there were hundreds of years ago, which is a pity, because according to eBay, where most of it comes from, there is a good demand for these tiny silver toys. Unfortunately, most of the eighteenth-century toys made by famous silversmiths of the day are now in either private collections or museums. In fact Her Majesty Queen Elizabeth II has a remarkable collection of miniature silver toys.

An online visit to Daniel Bexfield Antiques (http://www.bexfield.co.uk) will assist all collectors of silver toys and enlighten them on their value and give you a good idea of current prices.

The object of this book has been to enlighten the collector as to what is available today, yet show them what is still available if one is prepared to look around and pay the price of Georgian miniature toys and collectables. Good luck with your collecting.

Figure 8   Small tea set and tray belonging to the author; purchased September 2010 for £236; made in Birmingham, 1905, by Saunders & Sheperd;[9] width: 103 mm (4.3") inc. handles; overall height 40 mm (1.5"); the teapot is 1.3" high.

---

[9] Cornelius Saunders & Frank Sheperd entered the trade of silversmith in 1888 and obtained the London hallmark of the leopard's head in 1889. They were founded in London by Cornelius Desormeaux Saunders, Snr and James Hollings Sheperd. They became Saunders & Sheperd Ltd in 1899 and Saunders Sheperd & Co Ltd in 1916. They were active at Holborn Circus, London (1873–1902)

Illustrations

Figure 9   Miniature taper stick, detachable sconce and snuffer, M: Yapp & Woodward, Birmingham, 1847, 23gm, ac: Sep. 2010, P: £140. *AC.*

Figure 10   Victorian silver dog, typical of those made in Schoonhoven, Holland, mid 19th c, no markings, 11gm, ac: June 2010, P: £35, *AC.*

Figure 11   Silver bench, no markings. Dutch, possibly late 18th c, L: 231mm, 18gm, ac: Dec. 2010, P: £67, *AC.*

Figure 12   Coffee pot, made in Amsterdam in 18th c, numerous unrecognisable markings, H: 69mm, 39gm, ac: Jan 2010, P: £75, *AC.*

Figure 13   Miniature lamp designed as a child's compact, complete with powder puff, Birmingham 1912, H: 70cm, 41gm, ac: June 2007, P: £85, *AC*.

Figure 14   Dutch model of an elf with a barrel, no recognisable markings. Possibly made in Schoonhoven, 20th century. *Courtesy of eBay seller Mattachewey.*

Figure 15   Sleigh pulled by horse. Markings, FAL over a dot. All enclosed in a diamond. Made in Schoonhoven, Holland, poss. 19th c, L: 70mm, 22gm, ac: Mar. 2008, P: £35, *AC*.

Figure 16   Horse and driver pulling log wagon, silver, blackened with age and grime, no maker's mark, typical of toys made in Amsterdam, early 19th c, L: 90mm, 34gm, ac: Feb. 2008, eBay, P: £110, *AC*.

Figure 17   Large sleigh with driver. Pulled by two oxen and led by a man. Inside the sleigh are three figures inc. a woman with umbrella. The seat has red velvet upholstery, *c.* 19th c., made in Holland, figure '1' stamped on sleigh, town mark and maker's mark, L: 78mm, 51gm, ac: Feb. 2005, P: £60. *AC.*

Figure 18   Fine and rare example of 19th c. Dutch craftsmanship. Royal coach pulled by six horses. Marks: rampant lion, maker's mark and date stamp 1851. L 80mm, 83gm, ac: Nov. 2010, P: £300. *AC.*

Figure 19   Circus tableau showing a clown and a horseman about to jump a high wire. M: Leendert Hoogwinkel (1749– 1831), Dordrecht, Holland, 55gm, ac: Oct. 2009, P: £56, *AC.*

Figure 20   Horsedrawn water carriage for irrigation purposes inc. driver. No maker's mark, poss. early 20th c, Dutch, L: 80mm, H: 50mm, 33gm, ac: July 2005, P: £13, *AC*.

Figure 21   Riderless horse carriage. Markings: EPOSE FRANCE printed underneath, otherwise no markings, L: 74mm, H: 34mm, 26gm, ac: Aug. 2009, P: £14, *AC*.

Figure 22   Classic sleigh tableau, with mid 19th c Dutch marks, Dutch year letter O (1847) and 'xxx' mark. Maker's initials DR. L: 80mm, 37gm, ac: Nov. 2010, P: £90, *AC*.

Figure 23   20th c teapot, M: David Hollander & Son, Birmingham, 1977, H: 30mm, 12gm, ac: Feb. 2008, P: £25. *AC*.

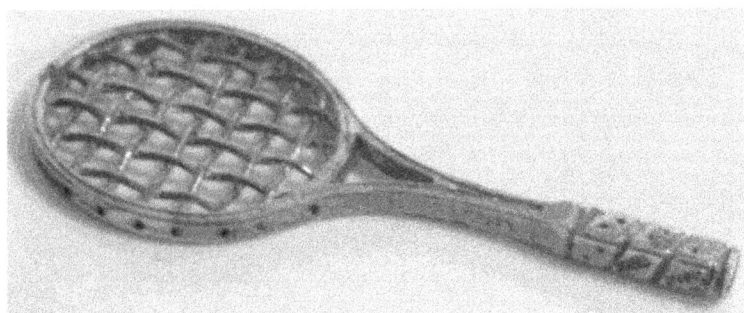

Figure 24   Toy tennis racket, no markings, L: 45mm, 2gm, ac: Dec. 2004, P: £5. *AC*.

Figure 25   Silver bowl, M: Horace Woodward & Co., Birmingham, 1884, 12gm, H: 24mm, ac: Nov. 2010, P: £40. *AC.*

Figure 26   Kettle on stand with burner, M: Levi & Salaman, Birmingham, 1905, H: 57mm, 16gm, ac: Sep. 2009, P: £85. *AC.*

Figure 27   Long silver tray with cups, saucers, cream, and sugar bowls, M: Saunders & Sheperd, Birmingham, 1905, L:140mm, 32gm, ac: Nov. 2009, P: £225. *AC.*

Figure 28   Miniscule 8-piece tea service inc. tea strainer and sugar tongs, M: Don Henry, Canada, 2010, L: 55mm, 28gm, marked, ac: Sep. 2010, P: £410. *AC.*

Figure 29   Displayed version of tea service in Figure 28.

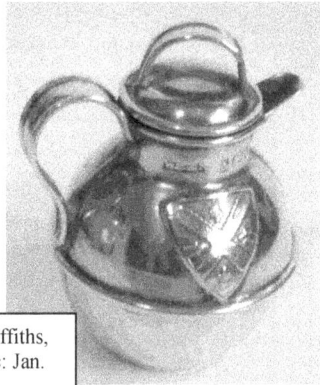

Figure 30   Jersey cream jug, M: W. Griffiths, Birmingham, 1904, H: 42mmm, 11gm, ac: Jan. 2009, P: £50. *AC.*

Figure 31   Three-piece tea service on tray, M: Saunders & Sheperd, Birmingham, 1905, 34gm, ac: May 2009, P: £230. *AC.*

Figure 32   Dutch miniature village musicians: 20th-century copy. P: €130. *Courtesy of Holland House of Silver Toys.*

Figure 33   Three wise men and moveable star, made in Holland. H: 90mm, D: 53mm, 45gm; similar version in V&A. Year mark **D** 1838, ac: May 2009, P: £148. *AC.*

Figure 34   Two-handled pot, Birmingham, 1927, M: unrecognised, H: 40mm, 9gm, ac: Mar. 2009, P: £40. *AC.*

Figure 35   Hanua silver watering can, imported, Chester, 1904, M: Samuel Boyce Landeck, 24gm, ac: Mar. 2009, P: £60. *AC.*

Figure 36   Pair of bedchamber sticks, Birmingham, 1866, D: 35mm, H: 15mm, 3gm, ac: June 2008, P: £132. *AC.*

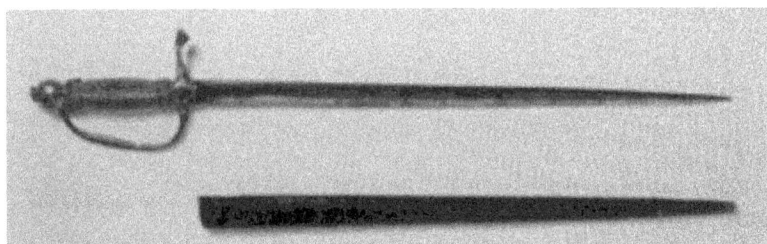

Figure 37   Lord Clapham's sword and scabbard, London, 1690–1700. *Courtesy of Victoria & Albert Museum.*

Figure 39   George III miniature teapot, M: Rebecca Emes & Edward Barnard I, London, 1809, H: 3.3", 116.8gm, valued at £2350. *Property of AC Silver Antiques.*

Figure 38   Miniature silver tankard, London, 1715–16. M: George Manjoy. *Courtesy of Victoria and Albert Museum.*

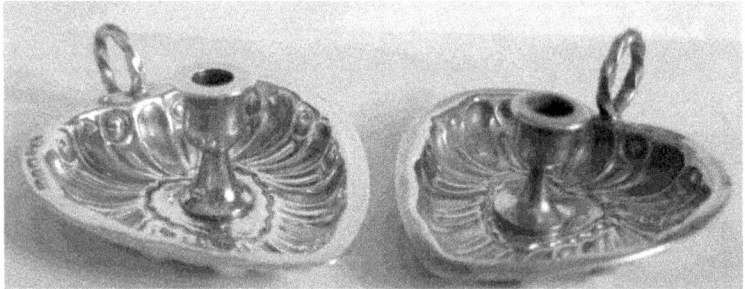

Figure 40   Pair of Victorian chambersticks, Birmingham, 1892. M: William Comyns, 14gm, ac: Feb 2011, P: £181. *AC.*

Figure 41   English miniature salver, London, 1709–10. M: David Clayton. *Courtesy of Victoria & Albert Museum.*

Figure 42   Walking the dog, Dutch, poss. Hoorn, no markings, typical mid 18th c, 8gm, ac: Nov. 2010, P: £34. *AC*.

Figure 43   Spinning wheel, Dutch, poss. Schoonhoven, no markings, mid 19th c, H: 53mm, 16gm, ac: Oct. 2009, P: £24. *AC*.

Figure 44   Dutch chair, 18th c, no markings, four similar chairs in V&A, H: 44mm, 9gm, ac: Mar. 2008, P: £40. *AC*.

Figure 45   Windmill, Dutch, mid 19th c, poss. Hoorn (renowned for their quality toy windmills) no recognisable marks, H: 80mm, 41gm, ac: Jan. 2011, P: £35. *AC*.

Figure 46   Sedan chair, probably Dutch, no markings (exempt), H: 43mm 12gm, ac: Jan. 2007, P: £48. *AC.*

Figure 47   Rickshaw with passenger, no details, H: 65mm L: 75mm, 30gm, ac: May 2009, P: £25. *AC.*

Figure 48   Miniature two-handled cup, London. 1714–15. M: William Looker. *Courtesy of Victoria & Albert Museum.*

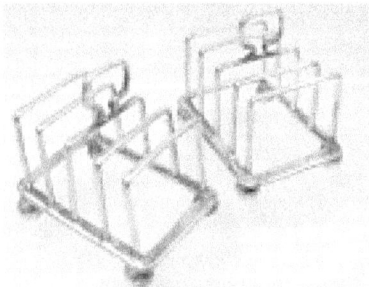

Figure 49   Pair of English miniature toast racks, Birmingham, 1919, hallmarked, 4cm x 6cm. P: £81. *Courtesy of Gwenysgems.*

Figure 50   Wicker basket, M: Montague Fiedlander, Chester, 1899, H: 65mm, 8gm, ac: Aug. 2010, P: £58. *AC.*

Figure 51 Brazier, Dutch, 18th c, poss. Schoonhoven, no markings, H: 28mm, 6gm, ac: Dec. 2010, P: £38, *AC*.

Figure 52 Sailing boat with crew, Dutch, poss. Hoorn, 1975. H: 120mm, 44gm, ac: June 2006, P: £78, *AC*.

Figure 53 Cup or trophy with lid, M: William Devenport, Birmingham, 1913, H: 78mm, 18gm, ac: Jan. 2010, P: £40. *AC*.

Figure 54 Modern model of 800 silver medieval mortar, marked, H: 45mm, 112gm, ac: Nov. 2010, P: £63. *AC*.

Figure 56   Miniature silver table, no markings, made in Dutch style, 17gm, ac: Sep. 2010, P: £57. *AC*.

Figure 55   Dutch tankard, 18th c, unfortunately over-embellished with Victorian cherubs, many marks on base, inc. import Chester, H: 52mm, 22gm, ac: Sep. 2007, P: £75. *AC*.

Figure 58   Miniature silver mug, M: Saunders & Sheperd, Chester, 1895, clear markings, H: 20mm, 3gm, ac: Sep. 2010, P: £40. *AC*.

Figure 57   Two-handled bowl, good quality, M: Mappin & Webb, Sheffield, 1897, Di (bowl): 60mm, H: 50, 64gm, ac: Jan. 2008, P: £47. *AC*.

Figure 59   English miniature saucepan, London, 1720. M: David Clayton. *Courtesy of Victoria & Albert Museum.*

Figure 60   Bucket, marked 900 silver, otherwise no markings, believed Irish, H: 55mm, Di: 55mm, 26gm, ac: July 2009, P: £27. *AC.*

Figure 61   Basket, Birmingham, 1901, no makers' mark, L: 79mm, H: 65mm, 32gm, ac: Sep. 2009, P: £15. *AC.*

Figure 62   Basket, Rotterdam, 19th c, D: 35mm, 18gm, ac: Oct. 2009, P: £81. *AC.*

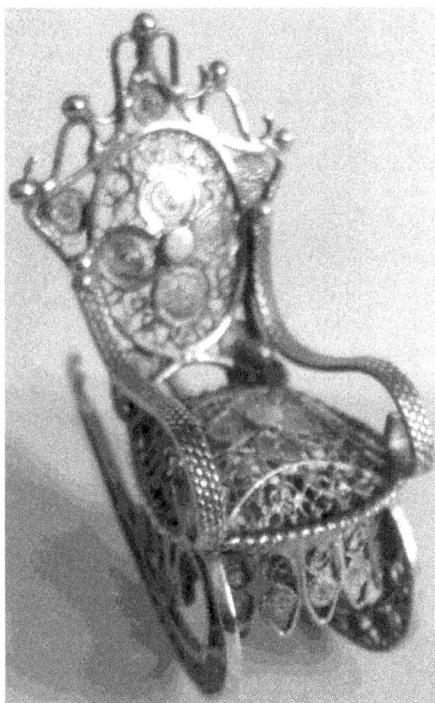

Figure 63   Magnificent filigree rocking chair, Continental, no markings (exempt), exquisite workmanship, H: 50mm, 11gm, ac: June 2008, P: £55. *AC.*

Figure 64   Tiny cut-glass Cayenne pepper bottle in silver frame, complete with silver cayenne spoon, M: Saunders & Sheperd, Chester, 1897, H: 60mm, 16gm, ac: Aug. 2008, P: £175. *AC.*

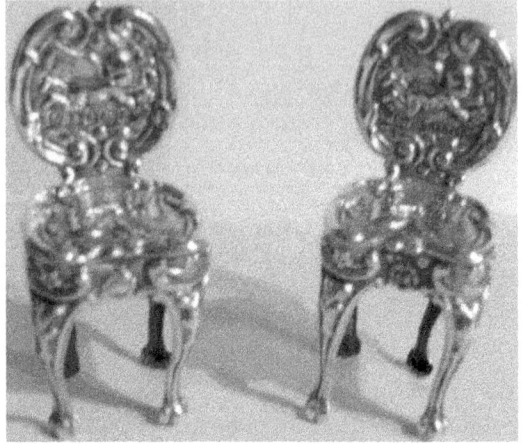

Figure 65   Two chairs, Birmingham, 1901, H: 42mm, 11gm, ac: Feb. 2007, P: £75. *AC.*

Figure 66   Pepper shaker, M: Levi & Salaman, Birmingham, 1897, H: 60mm, 23gm, ac: Oct. 2009, P: £44. *AC.*

Figure 67   Filigree sailing ship, no markings. H: 77mm, L: 80mm, 16gm, ac: Mar. 2011, P: £10. *AC.*

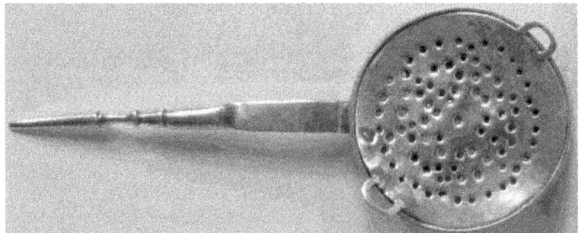

Figure 68 Dutch 19th c. preserving pan and cover, L: 115mm, 28gm, ac: Jan. 2010, P: £130. *AC.*

Figure 69   Table set, Amsterdam, marked 'xxx' and S2V; *cup*: D: 17mm H: 11mm, 4gm; *saucer*: D: 29mm, 7gm; *plate*: D: 32mm, 5gm; *spoon*: L: 45mm, 3gm, ac: Nov. 2010, P: £41. *AC*.

Figure 70   Dutch spinning wheel, poss. 19th c, no marks, H: 90mm, L: 80mm, 54gm, ac: Oct. 2010, P: £50. *AC*.

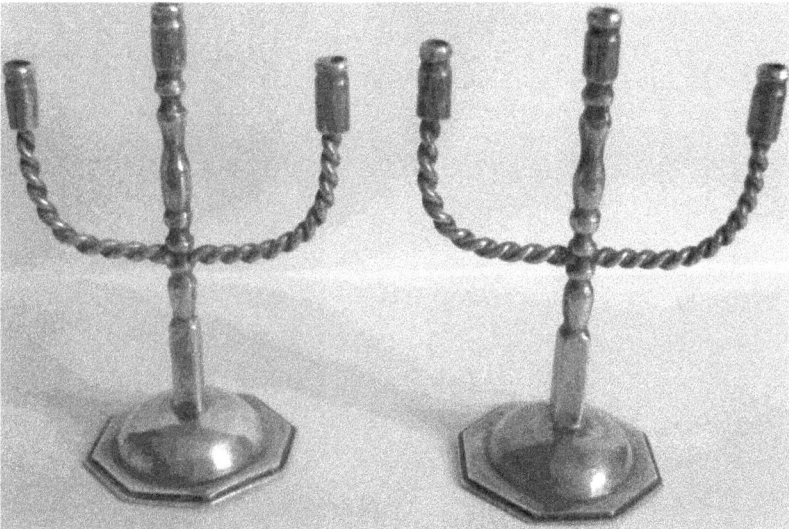

Figure 71   Pair candelabras, Amsterdam, 1905, maker's mark: single bushy top tree and sword, H: 47mm, W: 42mm, ac: Feb. 2005, P: £10. *AC*.

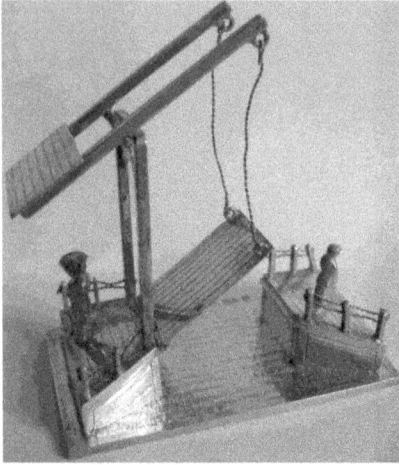

Figure 72   Dutch, manually operated bridge: date letter B = 1836, rampant lion, maker's mark (JV and hammer) all in rectangle, and a head facing left inside a circle; H: 90mm, L: 80mm, 71gm, similar version in V&A, ac: Sep. 2009, P: £50. *AC.*

Figure 73   Dutch model, 19th c, of man on toboggan; markings unclear. *Photo courtesy of eBay seller Eleanor.*

Figure 74   Dutch three-masted schooner in full sail with three crew, M: J. van Dijik (active 1901–39), Hoorn, 20th c, H: 115mm, L: 115mm, 51gm, ac: Aug. 2007, P: £75. *AC.*

Figure 75   Dutch two-masted sail boat on plinth, 20th century, probably Hoorn or Schoonhoven, marked 925 silver, L: 95mm, H: 114mm, 73 gm, ac: Jan. 2011, P: £75. *AC.*

Figure 76 Dutch snake cup, very rare, even as a copy, which this is. Made 1838. Clear maker's marks: two reversed crescents, but maker unknown. H: 47mm, 24gm, ac: Apr. 2011, P: £120.

Figure 77 Linen press, unmarked, 18th c, no markings; popular among Dutch silversmiths; examples by Arnoldus van Geffen, Daniel van Strant of Amsterdam, 1754, Jan Bonket and Abraham Effemans; H: 89mm, 32gm, ac: Jan. 2011, P: £120, est. value: £1200. *AC.*

Figure 78 Silver filigree platter, maker and country unknown, unmarked. ac: Feb. 2011, P: £30.

Figure 79 Dutch silver miniature teapot, Amsterdam,1767, maker's mark unclear, H: 45mm Est. auction value: £1000–£1500. *Courtesy of Christie's Images Ltd.*

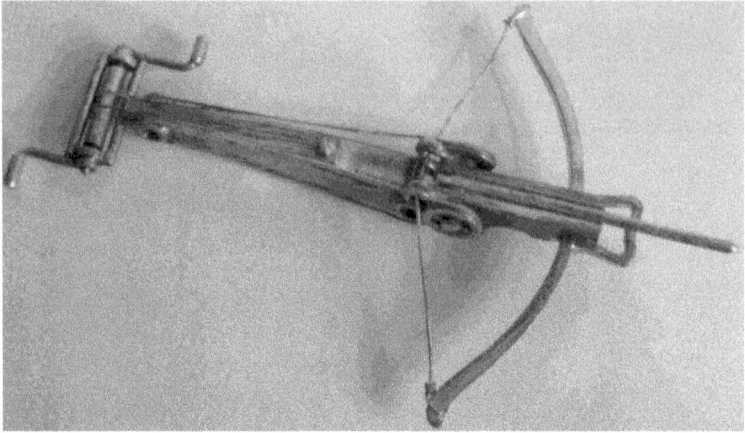

Figure 80   Crossbow, 800 grade silver, no makers name, ac: Jan. 2011, P: £110. *AC.*

Figure 81   Two modern silver chairs, hallmarks not clear, H: 63mm, 27 gm, £35. *AC.*

Figure 82   Dutch silver miniature coffee urn, early 18th c, marks unclear, on three scroll feet with three taps, est. auction value: £1500–£2500. *Courtesy of Christie's Images Ltd.*

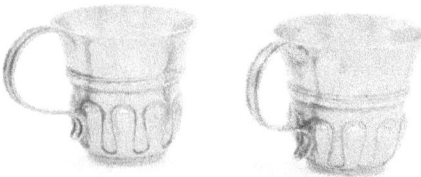

Figure 83   Rare pair of William III or Queen Anne Scottish silver miniature toy thistle cups, only one handle. Glasgow, c. 1700, mark of Thomas Cummings, original est. auction value: £2000–£3000. *Courtesy of Christie's Images Ltd.*

Figure 84   Dutch silver miniature teapot, Amsterdam, c. 1720. M: Fredrik van Strant I, est. auction price: £1200–£1800. *Courtesy of Christie's Images Ltd.*

Figure 85 Dutch silver miniature toy cruet stamped 10 with crowned circle, poss. 19th c. W: 88mm. Est. auction price: £1500–2500. *Courtesy of Christie's Images Ltd.*

Figure 86 Pot stand; marks on base: 6702 and three-legged table with number 800. Di: 45mm, H: 25mm, 21gm, P: £25. *AC.*

Figure 87 Dutch miniature Pijpencomfoo, 1737. M: Frederick van Trant II. Vendor's price: €2275. *Courtesy of Holland House of Silver Miniatures.*

Figure 88 Settee marked 'London, 1896'. Quite possibly **imported into this country from Holland** as it is stamped with the F import mark and has been embellished all over with babies and cherubs by a Victorian silversmith. Maker's initials appear to be RN. L:50mm, H: 55mm, 19gm, P: £65. *AC.*

Figure 89 Miniature silver coffee pot, London. M: David Clayton. *Courtesy of Victoria & Albert Museum.*

Figure 90 English miniature jug, London, 1688–89. M: George Manjoy. *Courtesy of Victoria & Albert Museum.*

Figure 91   Selection of miniature silver, London, 1720. M: David Clayton. *Courtesy of Victoria & Albert Museum.*

Figure 92   20th c English made coffee pot, part of a four-piece set, Sheffield, 1902, M: J & J Maxfield Ltd, who specialised in silver toys; H: 45mm, 15gm, ac: Feb 2010, P: £40.

Figure 93   Dutch working spinning wheel, markings: London, import, H: 77mm, 33gm, ac: Feb. 2011, P: £57. *AC.*

Figure 94   Dutch silver toy frying pan, 1750, M: Johannes van Somervil 1. Vendor's price: €950. *Courtesy of Holland House of Silver Miniatures.*

Figure 95   Dutch 18th c corner chair with London import marks, 1901. H: 33mm, 13gm, ac: Feb 2011, P: £47.

Figure 96 Dutch toy jug, c. 1810. Clear but unidentifiable markings on base. H: 47mm, 28 gm, ac. Feb. 2011, P: £35. *AC.*

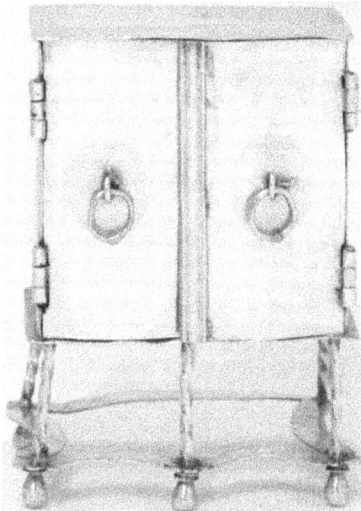

Figure 97 Cabinet on stand, London, 1703–4. M: George Manjoy.

Figure 98 Dutch horseless carriage, with passengers and driver. No markings, 19th c, 30gm P: £100. *AC.*

Figure 99 English condiment set, London, 1730–1. M: David Clayton. *Courtesy of Victoria & Albert*

Figure 100 Two-handled jug, Birmingham, 1918. M: Levi & Salaman.

Figure 101 Miniature spoon marked with owner's initials, L: 81mm, 3gm, P: £96. *AC.*

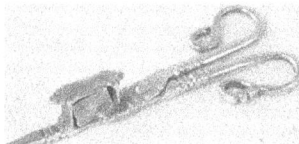

Figure 102 Dutch doll's house silver candle snuffers, c. 1740. M: unknown. Vendor's price €670. *Courtesy of Holland House of Silver Miniatures*

Figure 103 Silver miniature table, London, 1750, M: Edward Medycott. *Courtesy of Victoria & Albert Museum.*

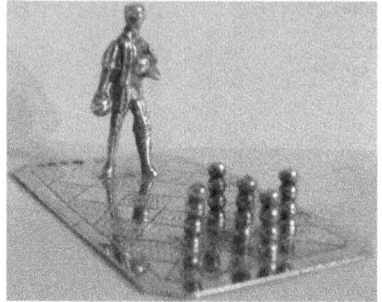

Figure 104 Dutch skittle player, possibly Schoonhoven, 1848.

Figure 105 Pair of miniature candlesticks, London. 1720. M: unknown. *Courtesy of Victoria & Albert Museum.*

Figure 106 Dutch toy tea kettle, 1765, Amsterdam, M: Master Arnold van Geffen. Vendor's price: €2100. *Courtesy of Holland House of Silver Miniatures.*

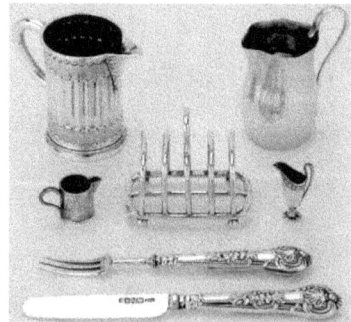

BEQUEST TO ASHMOLEAN MUSEUM, OXFORD, BY LADY HENRIQUES, 1953.

(Left) **Figure 107** Clockwise from top centre: 1. Coffee urn, Amsterdam, H: 7cm. 2. Silver miniature coffee urn on three legs, Amsterdam mark incorporating a letter N; maker's mark, Johannes Adrianus van Geffen (active 1766-98), H: 7.5cm. 3. Silver miniature spherical hot water urn on four-footed base, unmarked, H: 5cm. 4. Silver miniature coffee pot on three feet, Amsterdam mark uncrowned, H: 5.9cm. 5. Silver-gilt miniature coffee urn on three legs, marked 'AP', H: 6.1cm. 6. Silver miniature coffee urn on three feet, unmarked, H: 7.7cm.

(Right) **Figure 108** L-R, top to bottom: 1. Cylindrical jug with reeded sides, London, 1832–3, H: 5.1cm, M: Samuel Whitford II. 2. Plain jug, maker's mark: TC, H: 5.6cm. 3. Miniature silver jug, unmarked, H: 1.7cm. 4. Toast rack, London, 1833–4, M: Charles Rawlings and William Summers, L: 5.2cm. 5. Miniature silver cream jug, unmarked, H: 2.7cm. 6. Miniature silver fork, unmarked. 7. Miniature silver knife, Sheffield, 1832, M: Atkin & Oxley, L: 11.8cm.

Bibliography

Antique Collector (1975) *Silver Toys and Miniatures*, February 1975.

Delieb, Eric (1970) *Investing in Silver*. London: Corgi.

Greene, Vivien (1995) *English Doll's Houses of the 18th and 19th Century*. Overlook.

Heal, Sir Ambrose (1972) *The London Goldsmiths, 1200–1800; The London Goldsmiths, 1200-1800; a Record of the Names and Addresses of the Craftsmen, Their Shop Signs and Trade-Cards. Published Under the Patronage of the Worshipful Company of Goldsmiths of London*. Newton Abbot: David & Charles.

Houart, Victor (1984) *Miniature Silver Toys* (translated by David Smith). London: Random House Value Pub (original French edition, *L'Argenterie miniature*, published 1981).

Hughes, Bernard and Hughes, Therle (1973) *Collecting Miniature Antiques*. London: Wm Heinemann Ltd.

Jackson, Sir Charles James (1921) *English Goldsmiths and their Marks*. London: Macmillan & Co. Ltd.

Poliakoff, Miranda (1980) *Silver Toys and Miniatures*. London: Victoria & Albert Museum.

Wttewaall, B.W.G. (1987) *Klien Zilver 1650–1880*, Amsterdam: A. de Lange.

Appendix I   Museums to Visit

United Kingdom

Ashmolean Museum
Beaumont Street
Oxford OX1 2PH
tel: 01865 278002
www.ashmolean.org

Bethnal Green Museum of Childhood
Cambridge Heath Road
London, E2 9PA
tel: 020 8983 5200
www.alondonguide.com/bethnalgreenmuseumofchildhood.html

Manchester City Museum
The Manchester Museum
The University of Manchester
Oxford Road
Manchester M13 9PL
tel: 0161 275 2634
www.museum.manchester.ac.uk

Museum of Childhood
42 High Street
Edinburgh EH1 1TG
tel: 0131 529 4142
www.edinburghmuseums.org.uk/Venues/Museum-of-Childhood.aspx
Museum of London
150 London Wall
London EC2Y 5HN
tel: 020 7001 9844 0
www.museumoflondon.org.uk

Victoria and Albert Museum
Cromwell Rd
London SW7 2RL
tel: 020 7942 2000
www.vam.ac.uk
Windsor Castle (Queen Mary's Doll's House)

Windsor
Berkshire SL4 1NJ
tel: 020 7766 7304
www.windsor.gov.uk

Holland

Rijksmuseum
Jan Luijkenstraat 1
1071 CJ Amsterdam
Netherlands
tel: 020 6747000
www.rijksmuseum.nl/

Frans Hals Museum
Groot Heiligland 62
2011 ES Haarlem, Netherlands
tel: 023 5115775
www.franshalsmuseum.nl/

United States

Philadelphia Museum of Fine Arts
P.O. Box 7646
Philadelphia, PA 19101-7646
tel: (215) 763-8100
http://www.philamuseum.org

Yale University Art Gallery
P.O. Box 208271
New Haven, CT 06520-8271
tel: 203 432 0600
http://artgallery.yale.edu

The Art Institute of Chicago
111 South Michigan Avenue
Chicago, Illinois 60603-6404
tel: (312) 443-3600
http://www.artic.edu

Index

Note: page numbers in italics refer to illustrations.

About the author

William G. Jackman has been in the antique trade, buying, selling and collecting for 45 years. He has written numerous articles for the press and antique magazines, and has lectured on Georgian glass to dozens of Probus clubs, U3As, and other associations in the southwest of England. He is a member of the Glass Society, Silver Society and the Society of Authors.

This is Bill's second non-fiction book. His first, *Masonic Memorabilia for Collectors* (Gemini Publications Ltd, 2002), an illustrated price guide, has sold well all over the world. He has written and published four poetry books (all proceeds donated to charity) and has written plays and a six-part situation comedy based on caravanning. He has published one novel, *The Freemasons Daughter* (Authorhouse, 2009), and two further novels are in preparation.

Bill is retired and lives with his wife Jinty in Weston-super-Mare.

Visit online at:

www.mne-aesop.com/jackman

www.ingramcontent.com/pod-product-compliance
Lightning Source LLC
Chambersburg PA
CBHW051838040426
42447CB00006B/593